ARE YOU A GOOD LEADER?

GET THE 30 MOST POWERFUL LEADERSHIP TIPS, TOOLS & TECHNIQUES

'The Author of YOUR JOURNEY TO THE TOP'

REVISED EDITION 2023

RICHARD AHENKORAH

BlueRose ONE.com
Stories Matter
NewDelhi • London

BLUEROSE PUBLISHERS
India | U.K.

For permissions requests or inquiries regarding this publication,
please contact:

BLUEROSE PUBLISHERS
www.BlueRoseONE.com
info@bluerosepublishers.com
+91 8882 898 898
+4407342408967

ISBN: 978-93-5819-874-4

Cover design: Shivam
Typesetting: Namrata Saini

First Edition: November 2023

Dedication

To the victims of COVID-19 and also friends and families who lost their loved ones during the pandemic in 2020.

To the A-Team

My wife Sarah and my children: Keithania, Drusilla and Rain

To my best friend

Justice Kwame Konadu, 1979 - 2020. He was more than a good man.

Godspeed, my friend!

N.A.L.I

NEW AFRICA LEADERSHIP INSTITUTE

. inspire .

Acknowledgement

I express my deepest gratitude to everyone who contributed to this book- from start to end. I am always indebted to Ben Boateng, Samuel Addo and Adē bayo Samuel Ogunkoya.

Foreword

I have known Richard for over 10 years. During this time, we have worked together and shared the same office at some point; when he was the Head of HR at a financial institution where I offered my services as a retained Management Consultant in leadership, high performance, and team development.

Apart from our professional relationship, I have gotten to know Richard well in a personal capacity. We have travelled together on countless occasions to conduct leadership training, team development workshops, seminars, coaching and mentoring sessions for high-performing teams.

The key qualities of Richard that I admire most have been his honest commitment to excellence and his outstanding capacity to create incredible insights. Since I have known him, his dedication to professional development, leadership training, and personal growth has been remarkable. He never stops acquiring new knowledge, and skills, and constantly trying out new and ingenious ways of approaching situations to achieve the desired outcome.

I can say with confidence that Richard has been there. He has always identified talent, developed high-performing teams, and mentored individuals who have become great leaders. He has done the hard work and learnt the art of leadership with total dedication, now a master. He knows his stuff; and possesses an enormous wealth of knowledge and wisdom to share with all of us.

Today's environment is characterised by intense competition, new technologies, multi-generational workers, globalization, remote work teams, and stiff competition for top talent. At the same time, many organisations and institutions are underperforming, experiencing unsatisfactory employee engagement, and growing demand for higher pay and benefits. For an organisation to thrive and deliver exceptional shareholder value demands true leadership and absolute commitment from everyone. I can state emphatically that, this is the more reason why we need Richard's new book at this very moment.

Richard is an ardent believer in continuous professional development and has persistently been serious about giving his all to develop teams and produce results for his organisation. He has designed and conducted training programmes, shared insights, taught, and contributed to the success of many people in different organisations. I have seen him performing in his zone. In my long career to date, I have met a few leaders who have consistently demonstrated the passion and commitment that you will find in Richard.

Richard is right in asking the most important question – where is leadership? Even if we knew where they are, are they any good leaders? In every organisation or institution, people are sitting at the very top and are expected to lead but their attitude, behaviour, character, and more importantly their results, do not demonstrate that they are leaders. They are indeed dragging their organisations and institutions down through their lack of vision, clarity, attitude, integrity, and poor performance. They create a toxic atmosphere of demotivation and depress creativity and high performance. They forget that they must lead the people and fix the situations.

There could not have been a better time than now for Richard to share his depth of knowledge and experience in leadership to provide key proven tips, tools, and techniques to help many more people who are currently in leadership positions, as well as those who aspire to such positions to equip themselves to become real leaders who consistently deliver exceptional results through their teams.

Critical to achieving desired objectives, according to Richard, is the responsibility of the leader to set "SMARTER" goals, and lead with passion towards the realisation of the goals. He points out that as a leader, you must be laser-focused on the bigger picture. You don't blink. You don't get disturbed. You constantly keep the big-picture mentality during both good and challenging moments. No matter the situation you face, you remain resolute, and determined to stay on track.

You will learn that leadership is influenced through distinguished moral character and impeccable principles. No real leader cunningly manipulates the power naturally associated with the office he holds to dominate, undermine, and intimidate his people. To act in such a callous manner is a dangerous affront to leadership. Real leaders consciously build trust with the people. Consequently, the people become attached to these traits of the leader and are inclined to follow her, and work smart together to contribute to the vision and objectives established by the leader. In this genuine partnership, the leader unleashes the enormous potential in her people for them to develop their true capabilities and excel.

In this book, you will also gain a deep understanding of many practical steps in laying the right foundation, and establishing the appropriate culture for the team, or organisation. A culture and value systems enshrined in respect for inclusiveness and diversity, commitment to teamwork and high performance. Pertaining to performance, Richard has made it abundantly clear that leadership is all about getting things done. Period. There is no need to debate this. A leader has to produce and show the results. The resiliency in delivering results must be your hallmark as a credible leader. You choose to settle for nothing less than top performance through your people. Therefore coaching, mentoring, continuous development of the team, monitoring and instantaneous feedback become central to your leadership success. Your people see it in you, and they learn it from you. Together, you work as a strong team to achieve unimaginable results.

This book provides great tips and techniques on major leadership responsibilities including setting priorities, developing talent, performance feedback, motivation, succession planning, conflict resolution, and leading by example. In each of these areas, you will find specific practical techniques to sharpen your competence and gain ideas that will be of immense assistance to you when you must address them. You will find that he brilliantly uses memorable words and phrases that perfectly encapsulate the totality of the leadership technique in making its meanings and significance abundantly unambiguous. They include the Hot Stove Rule, Plus One Attitude, Tomorrow Today, Leader Nemesis, and Pathfinder.

One of the tips that resonates deeply with me is the Leader's Motive. It states that the leader must prove his capabilities by producing results. That's it. It is about setting goals, developing the people, motivating, empowering, coaching, mentoring, training, and guiding the people. A true leader takes full responsibility for her own actions, and importantly, for the results from her people. The buck stops with her.

A natural step from the Leaders Motive is another powerful chapter in this book called Build the People. In this section, Richard succinctly provides you with simple yet practical and effective tips to build the capacity of your people. I know team development to be one of his strong competencies. Therefore, I encourage you to dive into this section and pick up all the brilliant ideas available to you, to transform your team, and position it for high performance. He makes it plain that the onus is on you as the leader to always redirect the focus of the people to remain purposefully firm on the vision, objectives, and targets that must be achieved. When you lead your people with one common purpose and dedication to the shared goals, they practically believe that "no mountain is too high to climb and no river is too deep to swim in", according to Richard.

If you are ever told that leadership is a walk in the park, do not believe it. That's fake news. Here is the reason - Leadership is hard work, as stated by Richard in this book. I totally agree with him. Truth be told, nothing good comes for free, you must do the work to bring about the change and the results you seek. A true leader makes sure that his people understand this important principle. Through your dedication to the vision, and commitment to drive high performance; you get the team behind you and together you get to work. Pursuing mapped-out goals for your team or organisation is always not easy.

The great news is this. A credible leader knows that it will require hard work from everyone to get to the intended destination. In this book, you will learn that as a leader you will be in the spotlight all the time. Your every utterance, behaviour, and action will be critically appraised. Your results and accomplishments will be scrutinised too. There is no hiding place for you as the leader. This is what it is. An option you have is to learn from the terrific tools and techniques that Richard has shared with us in this book, so you too can consistently work hard with your people to deliver the results that exceed expectations.

I highly recommend this distinctive book to you. I know the true value of what you will learn from it and how it is going to shape your leadership skills and competence to unlock your potential and propel your career to become the forward-looking and great leader you are. I encourage you to start putting into practice all the 30 most powerful tips, tools, and techniques in this extraordinary book of leadership from today. You owe it to yourself, your team, and your organisation to lead with vision, passion, character, and integrity. You are in good company with Richard. Enjoy your beautiful journey to the top.

Ben Boateng

Managing Partner

Centre for Corporate Performance

October 2020, UK

Contents

Taster

I have led and I have followed. In both 'realms' there are lessons. In all situations I learned. One thing I've learnt for certain is that each circumstance is unique. In truth, identical situations are not the same, and similar situations may not be similar even in terms of leadership skills required to fix *same* situations. Heraclitus nailed it nicely *'no man ever steps in the same river twice, for it's not the same river and he's not the same man'.*

On my journey, I have always used the PEN. I know you can use it too. It has kept me going every step of the way. First, develop a lot of PASSION. Never run out. Next, gain EXPERIENCE. You can't put money on it. Sometimes experience comes the hard way. Yet take it as it comes. It is a very good friend. It's a checker and a teacher. Experience teaches fools, as said on the streets. Lastly, be NIMBLE. Be dexterous and quick to react to your environment. Dexterity makes you flexible to adapt to situations in a more positive way.

This is my PEN. I once took over a team as the Head of Region. My words were concise and compelling. I invoked the swim or drown mantra and more than eighty per cent of the employees were ready and willing to swim. Those who were not prepared to swim drowned. But a true leader would have to ensure that no one drowns.

As this book shares what sacrifice means in leadership, you'll come to terms that leadership is responsibility. Yes, some drowned. But I had to bring them up to speed and others were re-assigned to excel. Sometimes we cannot choose the music life plays but I know we can change the kind of dance. The dance floor is very big. Remember that, it can also get slippery, dirty and bloody. All you need to do is to learn to define your AREA on the dance floor. Know your Actors, learn to React maturely, know your Environment and be Agile with a clear destination in mind. Leadership is about breaking grounds. You can only break grounds if you know your terrain. This book will guide you to know where to go and how to go, in line with the rudiments of leadership. Just so you know, every step matters on your leadership journey. Don't miss the first to correct with the second. You may miss your steps, tumble and fall.

Learn to leave the stage when the curtain is drawn. You don't race with your shoulders, legs and the fact that you have stamina and tenacity to enjoy the last lap. To win or to lose is in the mind. If you want to have a clean home run, use your head. Learn to run to the end of the race. Build mental strength. Don't skimp on leadership goals. Drive yourself. Lead teams. Fix situations. This book will stimulate your thinking towards self-efficacy. I witnessed a 'crow' dead in an 'Eagle's Eyrie' and people thought the eagle overawed and killed the crow. People find themselves in places they don't fit, so they act up. To the point, you need to get ready for giant unimaginable assignments every step of the journey. After reading this book, you will learn to place value on every decision you take in leadership situations. This book is your pill. It may be bitter to assimilate at some point but you'll get better with it. This is your book. Read it. It's wisdom. It's worth more than jewels and pearls. The year 2020, paraphrasing Charles Dickens (Tale of Two Cities), was the best of times and it was the worst of times. 2020 taught us real lessons in leadership that the safest place to be is home. When you dive deep into this book you'll learn that home is where family is. A leader's family is the people he leads. There is no better time to publish this book. A time where leadership and learning are of utmost importance to problem-solving. This book subtly opens you up to the meaning of Service, Ownership, Agility and Respect. Are You a Good Leader? Get the 30 most powerful Tips, Tools and Techniques.

Introduction

Where is Leadership?

Leadership as a subject gets interesting by the day. Progressively, understanding leadership has brought meaning to the power of research and practice to academia and the workplace. In recent times, at least two million people search for Leadership every quarter of each year to gain first-hand insight into what leadership is and what leadership is not. The fact is, leadership is gradually becoming a mystery if not unfathomable. People can't find leadership. From the office to the churches and from politics to homes, leadership is gradually dissipating into thin air. I have had a stint in the corporate world from entry level to executive roles and my question remains; where is Leadership? I am not the kind of leadership authority who will ask, what leadership is. As a Lecturer of Strategic Leadership and Organisational Management and a Corporate Consultant for that matter, I will express my opinion, of course! My interrogation on leadership is to ask the question; where is leadership?

The world, institutions and homes are looking for answers. Don't be interested in scratching the surface if you want to understand the rudiments of leadership. Leadership is a multifaceted occurrence connecting the actions of a leader, the follower and the situation. To get tasks done effectively, efficiently and successfully, the leader must use the right models of motivation to stimulate follower actions to fix situations. Although leadership is about winning (Welch & Welch 2005); winning is not a destination. You have to win consistently. You have to unfailingly achieve or deliver set objectives. That is leadership. It's about mapping out strategies and showing character with courage and passion to lead a team toward a goal (even if you have to make ten attempts to win). It's tenacity. It is responsibility.

It's about seeing the light in the dark. This book should remind leaders to focus on the big picture. Leaders must learn and read to lead. A leader must be deep. Leaders don't roar at the seashore. They guffaw in the middle of the ocean. A leader blends the skill of being far and near. J.C Maxwell hinted that 'a leader must be close to the people and far from the people'. When you are close to the team, you learn from the team and they learn from you. You correct them and you shape them. When you are far from them, you hold the vision and you inspire them to follow you to greatness. The interactional framework that connects the leader, the follower and the situation can never be ignored in leadership success. Influencing is a skill. Leadership is influence (Maxwell 2005).

If you are still asking as I asked before; where is Leadership? This authentic work gives succinct answer to your question. This book will ask you not to look any further. Just read on! This book will build your leadership skills, interpret leadership actions and unleash your leadership abilities like never before. It speaks straight to your actions and inactions within leadership situations, team-building situations and governance opportunities. If you get equipped, share with the team and ask them to get copies. It is the vitamins to relevance at the workplace. This book will not only challenge you. It will change you. As a matter of fact, each chapter is a letter to you. This book serves you leadership as it matters when it definitely matters.

After reading this book, the reader must acquire the big picture mentality. Nothing can change in the absence of friction as far as leadership is concerned. Leaders shake tables and rock boats if they have to. Leaders should not replace organisational strategic goals and people development with self-motives. Leaders develop potentials by building the team's mental strength. Remember! You don't win with shoulders and legs. To win or to lose is in the mind. After all is said and done, leaders must be willing to leave the big stage when the show is over. Leadership is a learning process. This book provides the experience. This book will provide you with Leadership Tips, Tools, and Techniques. Read. Practise. Enjoy it!

CHAPTER

01

Paint It!

"You can change tomorrow if you don't like today"

*****

Leadership is one word that is constantly going through scrutiny.

It is fascinating rather than surprising. The point is, until leaders live to lead leadership remains ambiguous to me. Teams need leaders who will lead by the word! People have the urge but when they get into that space to exhibit leadership to the fullest, they blip. It is worth mentioning that, I will dig into the book authored by Hughes et al (2015). It gives a clue that people must begin to appreciate leadership to include the interactions between the leader, the follower and the situation. Fact! This starts the crucial process in appreciating what leadership really means. Many books define and subsequently describe leadership in many ways. I wish I could paint and take you through a mysterious journey on my definition of leadership. I see someone influencing others to do what art and science couldn't explain. That's leadership to me. I see someone gathered around by a team, and within the same expression, I see the same person within the same description moving ahead of the team and the people keep longing for him. This is a picture on my mind. The interesting thing within the picture is that the leader has the master-plan to induce the follower to fix situations and the followers are delivering on tasks not because they 'have to' but because they 'want to'. Which is why, I am inspired by Maxwell (2015) that everything rises and falls on leadership. How about Norman Schwarzkopf's provoking thoughts on leadership. He said and I quote 'leadership is a potent combination of strategy and character and if I have to make a choice, I'll go for the latter'.

Can you just look around and ask yourself; do people in high authorities either in politics or business have character? Yes character! I bet (not on my last coin though), you will find less than

25% who will show true character. Do not look very far because the base rate for bad leadership is between 50%- 75% (Hughes et al 2015). Leaders must have character. 21st century leaders must develop personalities worthy of emulation. The originality in a leader's personality must be edifying. A leader with leadership character must be a moral person with principles developed to serve. He must also be a moral manager who makes ethics unequivocal in all his dealings (formal and informal). As a matter of fact, a leader with the required character needed for leadership success must live the three key moral potencies: moral courage, moral efficacy and moral ownership (Hughes et al 2015). A leader must build fortitude to face his fears. A leader must own his words. Finally, a leader must be confident to overcome adversities. When followers don't see these traits and qualities in their leaders, they question the leader's judgement, decisions and character.

Most followers are following out of curiosity. They are not sure of the reasons why they follow a certain 'leader'. This is why most institutions are in a mess. Instead of leaders influencing teams to achieve desired goals, they exert power to please their whims and fads. In effect, followers are not inspired. Followers work in fear. Followers wished their leaders leave instead of wishing they live, and it's sad. Leaders need upgrade. Continuous learning. Leaders need new skills. Leaders need new ears to listen. Leaders should not just have eyes. Leaders need vision. Vision is foresightedness. Every leader must have one. A leader must see ahead and always see the end from the beginning, so to draw the future closer to the present and to run with the present to the future, having assessed the many corollaries of the journey.

Inevitably, there comes a time when the leader must leave the scene. It behoves on leaders to rethink and have a closer look at their legacy, their relevance and the opportunities they'll leave behind.

The only way to do this is to inspire confidence and show the way so leaders can reproduce their kind through the simple concept of mirroring. If the world can reproduce your attitude to evolve your kind to change the world positively, then you are on a beautiful journey to die so others can live.

You are a product of your past. Be conscious to invest in yourself today. Who you are today is as a result of the happenings and decisions of your past. You can change tomorrow if you don't like your situation today. You need to commit to good decisions today to change tomorrow. What you become tomorrow is also as a result of the decisions you'll make today. You'll be happy or sad today because of the decisions you made yesterday. As the stone rolls, you'll be happy or sad tomorrow because of what you'll choose to do today. Leadership is not only about legacy. It's also about relevance. Paint your vision.

CHAPTER

02

Laying the Foundation!

Leaders sow the seed for the next generation to reap.

*****

True leaders see beyond their lifetime. Leaders sow seeds for the next generation to reap. Any leader who sows seeds only to reap in his lifetime can be likened to a 'gold digger'. Visionaries sow for generations unborn. Leaders lay foundations. Laying a foundation is about selflessness (Munroe 2009). Laying a foundation involves people and thinking big. I mean developing people with diverse backgrounds, varying skills and different experiences. It calls for team buy-in and setting up a good climate for growth. I call it a good acceptable culture. Leaders must establish a culture to lay a good foundation. A culture that would be understood by all, lived by all and projected by all. Simply put, a leader establishes a team to live in harmony and respect. In laying a good foundation, a good leader makes room for trips and falls. As a matter of fact, don't expect a foundation laying process to be a simple workout.

Establishing a team's culture is one of the most difficult things to do in leadership development. If you don't get a team's culture right, forget about strategy. Peter Drucker hinted that culture eats strategy for breakfast. In my experience with team development, I can practically confirm that culture really eats strategy for breakfast, lunch, dinner and perhaps dessert. Culture makes and unmakes organisations. I have seen companies with good strategies failing to excel due to poor cultures. The beauty in laying foundations is to connect the dots of positive attitudes within a group. Remember, Ahenkorah (2018) hinted that attitude is contagious, be it good or bad. Every leader must shoulder the responsibility to build a strong culture in an organisation. Culture fades because of its adaptability but the stripes must be strong to remain relevant in trying times. The leopard cannot change its spots nor can the tiger change its stripes even if it lives in the sea. That is culture in its mean sense.

Laying the foundation is to define a culture and to set the base right and strong for take-off. Leaders must learn to build on rocks. The whole idea is that, you cannot chart a course with sweat, tears and blood and watch the base being grazed off. I have a corporate training topic packaged as Leadership Unusual couched by my training manager. It is about laying the foundations in organisational leadership which involves the five Ps and the other two Ps. Within the interactional framework, leaders struggle to fix situations when the issues become overwhelming. So leadership unusual focuses on keeping tabs on leadership and character as summarized in the Ps: People, Products, Pricing, Process and Philosophy which seeks to wrap the other two Ps: Policies and Principles of the organisation.

Obviously, you will need people to come along with you to lay a good foundation as a leader. 'if you want to go fast go alone and if you want go far go with people' as said. When you lay the foundation, think and learn to listen. Learn to pause a while even when you have the energy to keep going alone. Don't just do. Take your time and build a good foundation. Taking your time is not the absence of urgency. It's always crucial to build a corporate philosophy to guide the way employees think, behave and live. Lay a good foundation. Build a good culture to drive corporate strategies. Anytime you think of laying a foundation don't wait for another day. Do today. Think tomorrow. Think well and mean well. If you sow the wind you reap the whirlwind.

CHAPTER

03

Do it!

If you want to achieve something, do something. If want to achieve nothing, do nothing

*****

Leadership cannot be a noun. To lead is to do. Leadership must be a verb. It's simply a doing word. If you cannot get things done, don't put yourself up to lead. You can't win by doing nothing even though some argue that doing nothing sometimes, is a strategy. I won't wade in that debate, here. I'm yet to see a successful person who made it in life by sleeping. Leadership is beautiful, smooth on the top, rough at the edges and tough at the bottom. It's like the pebble. Tough and fine. When you lead, followers look up to you whiles the situation gazes in your face. Clearly, leadership is not a possessive word. It's an action word. It is a selfless venture. How to get things done requires a lot. You need to do things for others. Words are good. Words are kind. Action tops all.

Leadership is more than knowing. Leadership goes beyond saying. Leadership calls for doing. You can only do for the next in line to walk a mile in your shoes. If you want to achieve something, do something. Expect nothing if you do nothing. People don't follow people for nothing. Followers must have a reason to follow. The world is getting tired of sleep-walking leaders, if not, lazy leaders (to hit it right on the nail). It's gradually becoming a crazy world, where followers lead leaders and leaders rather follow followers. This is one of the main causes of leader-follower conflicts. Blanchard and Johnson (2003) hinted that a leader must be effective and a leader must lead for followers to follow. There is always a reason why leadership is best described and not necessarily defined. A leader must be tough and resilient. A leader just can't give up easily. In a VUCA world, things get volatile, uncertain, complex and ambiguous so leaders must learn not to be moved easily. To the point, leaders shouldn't be moved by situations. Leaders must rather move situations. It's either you move things or things will move you, in 21st century leadership. As a matter of fact, leaders must learn to be in control. When you are in control, you don't fight issues. You solve issues. When you are in control you don't confuse followers, you show them the way by guiding them to a preferred destination. When you are in control you don't fight followers and you don't strike them.

The 34th U.S.A President Dwight D. Eisenhower said, 'you don't lead by hitting people over the head- that's assault, not leadership'. Leadership is about maturity. It's about having a master-plan. It's about executing the plan. It's about delivering on your mandate as though there is a contract between the follower, the situation and the leader; because really, there is. It's about keeping your eye on the ball. Unwavering. It's not enough to clamour for a leadership role for role sake. Beyond the position is the work, commitment and sacrifice to produce results.

Leadership must be refreshed if not reformed. Some say being a leader is a lonely road. It shouldn't be, for a 21st century leader. Anytime you feel you are lonely as a leader, reengage the interactional framework to bring the follower, the situation and you, to the fore. There will forever be an interesting relationship between the leader, the follower and the situation as far as leadership is concerned.

CHAPTER

04

Live it or Leave it!

Wake up and smell the coffee

*****

Leadership is partly science. Leadership is partly art. A little bit of this and a little bit of that. Sounds like a rhyme but it's not, entirely. In Organizational Leadership, actions of Leaders are being measured and thus Leadership must be felt. I once followed a Line Manager who always said 'let the followers follow you, don't follow the followers'. It's good to be close to your team but it's crucial to be far from them. It's a skill. As hinted, a leader is one who's close to the people yet far from the people. Not confusing, right. A leader must stay close to the team to coach, to train, to share, to care and to attend to the needs of the followers. When you are close to the followers, you can monitor them and when you are far from them, you can inspire them. When you are always close to them there won't be any path to follow but when you are far from them there is always a motivation to follow. Being close and far with the team is to coach, mentor and to lead the team.

Munroe (2009) implied that leadership is an attitude. In simple terms, live it or leave it. This rocks! Let me share this secret with you and promise never to tell anyone. There's nothing to lose in leadership. There's everything to give and to gain in Leadership. Empower followers. Here, leaders must learn to delegate to the team and also invest time and resources on the team to build capacities and expose followers to new techniques and newer ways of getting things done. There is nothing like giving power to the ones who need them. Learn to give power to the followers so to gain influence. Build trust. You can build trust within a team when your vision is always clear, when you empathise with the team, when you are consistent in your deliverables and more importantly, when your integrity is untainted and unquestionable. At the office, for example, delegate, promote, elevate, motivate, gratify, correct, learn from the team and develop followers. I mean grow leaders. Create a leadership pool. Give power to the team.

As a CEO of an institution, you don't necessarily need any power to move any of the company's vehicles around, for example. Yet a junior colleague needs your approval to move a certain vehicle around. This is because you have the power and the follower needs the power. This is the main reason why a leader must not focus on power because the leader has the power. As followers long for power, leaders must yearn for influence. There are many influencing tactics applied to balance the art and science of leadership. Leaders must build trust within teams anytime, any day. This gives influence. It may take time to build trust, nonetheless, it is the golden key required to solve leadership challenges. When you are trusted, you can easily mobilize the team to fix situations. Of course! Beyond trust is competence. When you are trusted and you are competent it's a beautiful experience as a Leader. With the right space, a motivated team, trusted people, good system, beautiful culture, clear vision, good values, sound objectives, realistic mission, good working strategy, and a structured organ, a Leader will be seen as effective. It is so because the Leader will be combining the expert and referent powers with a good balance to lead.

Being effective is to show high concern for people and high concern for results. Don't be interested in the position as a Leader. That is the least of the levels in leadership development. Be interested in developing the next Leaders. It is leadership, when you develop a leader and that leader develops another leader. Be interested in changing situations and fixing them as well. Be fascinated in keeping the clock turning and moving teams and organisations from a certain level to a defined destination. Establish values and live it. Every follower does what the leader does, unconsciously or subconsciously. Leaders must develop the art and science in leading teams. Leadership is hard work. Leaders must simply wake up and smell the coffee. There is no walk in the park and tyranny is not sustainable in 21st Century Leadership either.

CHAPTER

05

Look Until You See

...measure your words or your words will measure you

*****

Often times, we look but we don't see. In leadership development, you need to look until you see. It calls for full-time 'looking'. A leader must learn to look, think and see- LTS for short. Allow the mind to wander a bit though focusing on the outcomes. Always learn to see the end from the beginning or as *Covey (1999 p.97)* advises, begin with the end in mind. Keeping your eye on the ball is a full-time job. It has never been a job for the uncommitted, anyway. Understand your area. Think. Be curious to see through the crystal ball even if it reflects contrasting lights. Learn to understand the communication process. When you do, listen with empathy. Know how to rally people around to see in the same direction. Saying what you want to say is very crucial here.

When looking, learn to listen to the sounds, including the silent noises. Silent noises are always fuelled by leader actions. They are always the elephant in the room. But if you look well and you listen well, you will think well, you will see well and thus you will communicate well. If you look and you listen, you learn to interpret voices even if they are not silent noises. If you learn to look deep at a wall, staring closely into it, you'll surely see through it.

There's no point enjoying speaking and getting excited for applauds when you haven't looked and seen the situation in question. This reminds me of the first time I heard of the expression 'laughing through your teeth'. I guess I was six, then. For some reason, I fell for that expression. Leaders must learn to spend time with problems. Look through the problem until you see the problem. Seeing the problem and understanding the issues present a solution. Change the spectacles if you cannot see through the lens.

Every part of a leader should communicate and resonate positive actions. Look at problems until they start looking at you. I mean confront problems. Sometimes it's okay to rock the boat. When speaking, measure your words or your words will measure you. Don't be quick to say the things you cannot do because followers will demand them at the appropriate time. Zeno of Citium hinted that it is better to trip with your feet than with the tongue. When the glass bottle drops on a hard surface, manage the noise no matter how loud it smashes. Managing sound is a skill. Controlling the wind calls for higher skill. Cleaning up the mess calls for courage.

Even when you don't have the full support, you can still smash the ceiling if you have to. It still comes back to looking and seeing. Focus. Sometimes you can focus on the wrong things that can take a lot of energy from you. Yet don't worry much. There's always room for a U-turn if you are ready to learn and get things back on track. Leaders appreciate every hill and valley. The key thing is to observe all the things you see at every point of the journey.

When you want to develop the art of seeing in Leadership, don't bother much about those who are for you and those who are not. Sometimes it's fine to keep a small circle. Come with me and let's argue it out. *Inspired by Collin Powell's Spiral of Experience (Hughes et al 2015)*, sometimes the things you see affect your perception and they make you reflect on the things you've seen and those you perceive. After a good reflection, you become selective of what you've actually seen which can ostensibly affect what you intend to see.

Good leaders will let followers see what they want them to see. All they need to do is to influence followers to look until they see. Good CEO's know that an employee with a bad attitude will make a good customer lose interest in a great company with good products, good services and the best people. With this in mind CEO's don't stop shaping mind-sets. This is why good CEO's keep the focus as the course.

CHAPTER

06

Sifting

Anytime you feel like stopping, think of why you started

*****

A very good friend gave me a present. An hourglass! Anytime I look through it, I see myself going through a process. A process of scrutiny. Maybe that is the power of the glass. Every Leader goes through sifting. Making your vision clearer in blurry moments is a skill. Ahenkorah (2018) shared that your vision shouldn't blur even in tears. Leaders must be unfaltering to sift no matter what it takes.

Categorise by prioritising your options and make decisions on the go. Don't leave any area grey. To live or to die is to decide (Ahenkorah 2018). If you learn to sift, you learn to make the right decisions. There's no point throwing the baby away with the water and dancing around that you successfully 'threw' the water away. How about the intern surgeon who said that the operation was successful because he got the baby out even though the mother in labour died in the process.

Sifting comes with responsibilities and leaders must be ready for this. Learning to give a good account of your performance and measuring the team's progression feed into sifting. Leaders must use the feedback loop. It works. Seeing the distance of a journey and celebrating your arrival gives a sign of winning but it also calls for sifting so to guide your steps. In sifting, a leader must focus on the outcome, with a clear understanding that every process or milestone is as important as the final outcome.

Anytime you feel like stopping when sifting, think of why you started. There's not much incentive in sifting. It's a self-motivating process. Learn not to stop even when it hurts. You'll definitely smile after the process. Harrell (2005) affirms that we always have the power of choice. It is worth reiterating this point because good leaders listen

(Empathy: HBR Emotional Intelligence series 2017). They listen. They listen very well. They listen to the end.

In reality, great leaders listen to 'rubbish' too. To the point, great leaders allow followers to speak their minds, and some followers really 'speak their minds'. Leaders must learn to sift. It is a skill to be tactful with priority when sifting. The only advice is that, sift because you have to. Sifting involves learning to tell it right in the face and not containing yourself in the grapevine. You don't have to hide behind people's shadows to sift.

Still staring through the hourglass I see solutions and I feel the weight of every 'sand' drop. Sifting makes vision clearer from a leader's own experience through an analytical perspective. What I'm not sure of, is the leader's sifting motives. If you sift and still have the grains mixed with the chaff, then the process must be revisited. A leader's sifting motive is always crucial.

If Goleman (2005) asserts that the body has a mind, then as a leader, you have every reason to look into yourself until you see through your body in an attempt to interpret what you sift for. It is always important to learn when to sift and how to sift in order to apply the mind appropriately on what to sift for.

CHAPTER

07

Gathering

Leaders gather great minds. Be the lead. Not the lid

*****

After sifting, a leader gathers. To gather is to collect and develop.

Gathering is not about putting a team together and watching them grow. It's about deliberately and consciously forming a team to grow and showing them the way. Put a team together, nurture them and leave them to shine. I mean learn to move on and teach the team to live for others. Someone is sitting in the shade today because someone planted a tree a long time ago. I didn't say this. Warren Buffett did just as others said. In every good institution, leaders work hard to shape the minds of followers to think in a certain way, which is why Leaders must learn to gather after sifting. Leaders must get the process right, hire right, place right and motivate right.

In gathering, leaders must learn not to overstay. Of course 'overstaying' is relative which is why good leaders have timelines and milestones. The argument is not to say that leave after you gather. Just don't overstay. Simple. Learn to leave so others will grow. Be the lead and not the lid. In looking out for successors don't bother to shake the table. Sometimes take the team to the high seas and rock the boat a little bit. How about using the rough road instead of the high-speed lane? In gathering, institutions must be courageous to develop new leaders when existing leaders fail at meeting and delivering established corporate objectives. That should, however, not be the basis for leadership development and new leader grooming initiatives. Development, here, involves capacity building and growing talents. Grooming is about coaching and mentoring employees to feed into an institution's succession planning programme.

It must simply be clear that leaders nurture followers not because previous leaders failed. Leaders nurture followers because of the responsibilities that lie ahead. The future is too promising to benchmark with past failures. Leadership is forward-looking. That's the foundation of gathering. Leaders gather great minds and leave them to live. This is Leadership. I never heard that a legend stayed on. But I hear a legend lives on. The legend lives because he achieved a certain milestone. Leadership is calling for a deliberate leave without overstaying. This is not an argument to say that societies don't have living legends. It is simply motivating for leaders to hit milestones to set new targets on their journey so new leaders will emerge.

If leaders learn to demand generational performance from followers everyone will think of doing more for the next generation and the world will build selfless leaders. Good leaders for example demand exceptionally high performance from every member of the team. In every institution, leaders must learn to demand more because every individual has the capacity to do more. In gathering, know that everyone matters. The ability to put different minds together makes one team different from the other. Gathering sets the tone for teamwork and preparation for take-off. Every level in team development requires fresh fuel as far as gathering is concerned. Constant team communication, frequent team briefs, consistent focus on the target, continuously measuring performance and deliberate calibration of team development are all part of the gathering process. Inasmuch as a good planning process passes for a good take-off, leaders must inch it up by organising team strength and aligning them with opportunities.

Gathering is about imparting values (Dotlich et al 2006). When you onboard a team member, share the concept of gathering. Gathering is also about preparation. Gather and let the team's attitudes be in sync with the organisation's values. Let the core or shared values be felt, let it be seen and let it be said. Let it be written and let it be known. Let the team go through the experience. In gathering, create a corporate culture within which the followers experience the shared values. Open your ears and eyes to team feedback. Don't get too excited. Gathering is also about getting-together. Have a do when you gather and don't forget that you gather to progress. Henry Ford was emphatic (Jakes, 2017) that coming together is a beginning; keeping together is progress; working together is success.

CHAPTER

08

Viewpoint

Don't be scared of your past when tomorrow is part of your future

*****

There is no point to gather if you fail to shape follower viewpoints.

But you can shape viewpoints if you personally have a good standpoint as a Leader. I read a book on how the world's best firms develop leaders for succession and business sustainability (Dotlich 2006).

They build the mind, the passion and the confidence of ordinary employees to become captains. They do this through succession planning initiatives and programmes with the aim to consciously change employees' mind-sets to entirely change employees' viewpoints. My takeout from the book remains, change mind-sets to change viewpoints. Leaders must learn to change mindsets through a mind-shifting process. When this is achieved within an organization, the institution can deliberately move to the next stage of creating a bench for good succession. Remember that you win matches from the bench as a leader. When an entire team sees through the same lens, the institution's viewpoint will be aligned.

Let me share a simple analogy on viewpoints. A young man from a clothing retailing shop was sent out to sell flying ties to a group of people living in the countryside. He came back and said to his Line Manager that the people living in the countryside are not exposed to urban life so he couldn't sell a single flying tie. That was an objective report empirically backed by facts. The Line Manager sent another sales officer to the same area and he came back with a report that simply read 'the people in the countryside don't wear ties. I mean none of them had one. So as a clothing retailing shop, my findings reveal a massive opportunity for us. We need to get in with more flying ties before our competitors do. As a retailing shop, we need to make sure we sell at least one to each of them because ours is to sell and theirs is to buy'. Viewpoint.

I have a personal example. When I started working as a career banker in Ghana, I had no network as a business development officer because I was out of the country for some number of years (studying and living in the UK). Most of my colleagues I returned to Ghana with resigned, because they had no network to build a good portfolio. True. But that cannot be a fact. My viewpoint was, thank God I have no real network. At least, I now have an opportunity to build one. People don't like to build. In 21st century leadership, have a disposition of a CEO at all times. Always wear a sharp and positive viewpoint backed by analysis, practice and creativity.

Even as you prepare yourself for leadership development, you should have a disposition from the top. Occasionally have a view from the top. It's not coincidental to see the offices of CEOs at the top floors in corporate settings. Having the bird's eye-view sets you apart always. Jakes (2017) hints that you must learn to see issues from the top before you start dealing with them.

Learning to be responsible for a process, an initiative or a mission at the workplace, makes you a master of that process, initiative or that mission. Learning to be responsible for a group of people gives you the natural influence to lead them. When you gather, you shape viewpoints.

In shaping your viewpoint, you shouldn't be scared of what might have happened in the past when you know tomorrow is definitely part of your future. Your viewpoint today, shapes your future tomorrow.

Leaders must work on the possible internal conflicts between leader viewpoints and leader motives because Leader viewpoints are influenced by Leader Motives. If the motives are wrong the viewpoints would be flawed. The reverse is true.

CHAPTER

09

Leader Motives

Don't keep on talking. Just prove it!

*****

There's always a basis for a leader's actions and inactions. When leaders mean well or they don't, it's not about what they say. It's about what they do. This is critical because people vary in their motivation to lead. Beyond conception and saying, there must be action backed by a commitment to follow through to the end. Whether leaders are selfless or selfish, it's always in their deeds. Don't be quick to measure what they say. Wait and measure what they do. So there is a thematic apperception test that seeks to project personality experiments to assess leaders need for power (Hughes et al. 2015). Some leaders personalize power and others socialize it. The greatest gift of every leader is to make the world a better place for the next generation. I once had a line manager who said it right in my face 'I'll show you where power lies'. Honestly, I felt sad for him. That is when I got to know that he didn't know he always had the power.

This is my take. Leaders should crave for influence and not power. Because, they have the power. What they always don't have is the influence. Unfortunately, power is transient. Influencing is lasting. Munroe (2009), Welch (2005), Hughes et al (2015) and Maxwell (2005) suggest that leadership is about legacy. But when it comes to leader motives it must inch a notch higher. It's also about relevance, when the motive is right. Leaders must create a good and sustainable ambience for others to grow to realize their dreams and potential. So leadership is actually not about the leader. Leadership is about others and the situation. Empower others and make them relevant to apply themselves for leadership success.

The fact that you crave for power to lead doesn't necessarily mean that you would be successful as a leader. Some leaders fight for power, they win power and they use power impulsively because they forget that their strength lies in their influence and not in the power. As long as people vary in their motivation to lead a team, an organisation or a country, their deeds will surely give them away as selfless or selfish. To the point, not everyone wants to lead and not everyone can lead, anyway. But the myth has also been demystified, interestingly, that everyone can lead. One beautiful statement I always hear from politicians in particular; 'I didn't want to lead, but my people said I have to lead'. This is pathetic and I guess it's not true either. Because a leader would have to go through a process which involves self-assessment, the least. A leader must answer the simple question. Why do I want to lead? If your answer does not point to solving a particular problem that would turn the fortunes of a team, an institution or a country around, forget it! If you can't be true to your followers, at least be true to yourself. Look into the mirror and ask yourself over and over again about your intention to lead and how it would motivate the followers to fix situations. To be an effective leader, the motive must be clear, without malice and it must be known. Don't keep on talking. Act. Don't be going around saying and saying. Show it. Enough of the promises. Just prove it.

CHAPTER

10

Responsibility

A leader must not leave anyone behind

*****

Leadership is about responsibility. To lead a team means your followers have transferred their worries to you. Yes, worries. This is actually so because followers have voluntarily renounced their rights to lead themselves to you so you can lead them as they follow. As long as people follow, the leader has a responsibility to take them home. Ahenkorah (2018) hints that the sheep may go astray but they want to get home, anyway. In effect, the shepherd shouldn't think his sheep are clueless or aimless. Followers also have a plan. It is, nevertheless, believed that the leader has a smarter way which is why they are given the rod to lead so followers would follow. It is for this matter, that a leader must be responsible. An effective leader converts his worries into thinking. Of course, 'uneasy lies the head that wears the crown', Shakespeare hinted. There's also a brighter side though. A leader needs not to be apprehensive wallowing and wading in fear. It is a beautiful place to be if you are responsible for others. All you need to do is to do what you are expected to do. A leader must ensure no one fails. A leader must not leave anyone behind even when a follower wants to.

Everyone knows what to do but few really get things done. Knowing and doing are two separate things. Being responsible is really about doing. On the flipside of things, to be responsible means a task must be done and when you fail to do it or you do it wrongly you are irresponsible. The world is getting tired of leaders pointing fingers at followers and situations. Human beings are collectively forgiven when people show honesty and willingness to learn.

A true leader always own all the failures as his responsibilities and blames no one nor provides any excuses as justifications. The key challenge is that followers are tired of leaders who do nothing and are not ready to learn either.

J.F Kennedy said leadership and learning are indispensable to each other (Hughes et al 2015). If you study the life of JFK, apart from his charisma, one thing stands out. He was always willing to learn. This gave him the privilege as a trusted and courageous leader (Dallek 2018). Remember, trust deepens influence not power.

In leadership, the shepherd must be responsible for the sheep. That's all. Although it's a tough one, the clue is that, when you look after your team your team will look after you. This is why leaders who look after institutions, are also looked after by those institutions. Leaders must commit to building organisational ambassadors and an organisational army if not organisational citizens. So one of my CEO friends in a discussion said to me, I have been responsible for my team all this while but they still give me away. Sad, isn't it. I encouraged him not to worry because it is part of leadership. So I introduced him to learn the art of empathy. Within responsibility is empathy. Learning to be responsible for others is a skill and an attitude for leadership development. Look after your people. Your team will never care that you know until they know that you care as J.C. Maxwell advises. Look after the business and administer every asset. Using the Ocean's Five Factor Model of Personality Types (Hughes et al 2015), get to know your team's individual personality traits, test their aptitude and cognitive skills, demand performance from them in line with their Job Descriptions-JDs- and Key Performance Indicators-KPIs, reward and punish as they learn to account for their stewardship. Ensure every asset is fully utilised because you are responsible for every asset's performance.

Responsibility comes with the capacity to accommodate sometimes unreasonable demands and also learning to manage egos and follower tantrums. Nevertheless, it is actually a beautiful experience to be responsible for a whole team's successes and failures.

Responsibility must be a lifestyle as a Leader and your every move must point towards ownership. You have the obligation to look after your people, processes and tasks. In effect, a true leader leads his people, processes and tasks to succeed. When you fully imbibe the concept that responsibility is a lifestyle, you'll always tune into improving yourself, followers, processes and tasks around you. To be responsible requires a lot of emotional intelligence too. You should be alert to align your thoughts to your feelings so you can align your followers' thoughts to their feelings for smooth people management outcomes. This is a skill to crave, in leadership.

As a matter of fact, leaders feel uneasy to shoulder destinies of irresponsible followers. The apprehension should however be positive. To be a responsible leader, you must learn to constantly calibrate by providing solutions and showing empathy, rewarding excellence and providing appropriate sanctions for deviance. To be responsible, you need to have firm control over situations and be on the move to chart a new path for followers to follow with minimal resistance. It's not a bad feeling to be nervous sometimes as a leader. It's actually great to feel overwhelmed with issues. Just have control of yourself, your situations and your followers. When the actions of your followers make you feel underwhelmed, embrace that as well. Submit yourself to be accountable to your successes and your failures. Show interest in individual and collective goals.

To be responsible, you need to be there for the team. When you are there for the team, listen. When you listen, act!

CHAPTER 11

Something Must Give

Be responsible for the pain so you can swim in the gains

*****

The more you appreciate the concept of responsibility and power in leadership, the more you tend to give yourself away just so you submerge your ego in the spout of your followers. But the upside is to ensure that you lift your people to follow you. Leadership is about dedication, commitment, accountability, stewardship, concern for people, concern for production and more importantly, sacrifice. In leadership, something must give. Sometimes leadership is about martyring and giving yourself away to have it back in pursuit of results. Effort is not enough in 21st century leadership which is why leaders won't stop pushing for results (Covey 1989). In effect, it's good to try but it's all about doing. No long talk. This is the main reason why I see leadership as a verb and not a noun. In pushing for things to be done, something must surely give. There is always a trade-off and it must be felt. Leaders must learn to live for others. Leaders must commit to teams and must commit to fixing situations. A leader must learn to give and leaders must teach followers to give. If leaders don't do this, followers grow without knowing how to give. Giving is about sacrifices. Leaders must develop the passion to give because a leader must learn to have a beautiful heart (Goleman 2005). From negotiation to decision-making, something must give. If you want to have a home run, learn to hit harder and to run faster.

At the workplace for example. Leaders must find a way to let followers know that the work environment is a serious space and not a circus. Leaders must seriously communicate this intention verbally and non-verbally. Nonetheless, that should not exude fear but should motivate and exhilarate employees to become better versions of themselves. Leaders must create what I call positive anxiety at the workplace so everyone will contribute to performance in an exciting and challenging way.

Every decision starts and ends with a leader's viewpoint. What happens in the middle of any decision process is just to keep the meal cooking well. To give, a leader must avoid being cocky and shouldn't appear weary. A leader must focus, motivate, inspire and act (Ahenkorah 2018, Maxwell 2005). In leadership development, a leader shouldn't blame situations and followers if projects and deliverables fail. A leader should take up the blame and fix it. A Leader doesn't give situations too much colour. It may be tough but the leader's responsibility is to fix it. Giving is about sacrificing.

Societies can't raise leaders if citizens are not willing to sacrifice. The workplace cannot raise leaders if management can't sacrifice. Of course, don't dream of becoming a hero if you can't sacrifice for your team. Sacrifices come with pain but there's happiness on the other side. Sacrifice now and enjoy its fruits later. I have had the privilege to have walked on the streets of some cities in West Africa and I learned a street lingua that 'no pain no gain'. It feeds squarely into 'something must give'. Be responsible for the pain so you can swim in the gains. If you learn to live more for the team, followers will 'die' for you and if you decide to 'die' for the team, followers will live forever for you. Learn to die for the team to live.

When you give more to the team you become 'extinct' and powerful; and that is leadership. In serious institutions, CEO's must enforce knowledge transfer. I enforce and endorse mentorship. I enforce and endorse giving. I ensure my workforce learns to celebrate themselves and their colleagues. These are actually fed into the institution's system and strata so that everyone learns to give something, from knowledge to gifts. Teams must be taught to sacrifice for others. I can't raise the next managers in my team if the members within the team are not ready to sacrifice. Something must give. It's a demand.

CHAPTER

12

Pathfinder

No doesn't mean Never!

"The imaginary thought of the final destination whets the appetite for continuous calibration"

*****

I remember the very first time I heard the word 'Pathfinder'. I was nine. It was a family trip to the countryside on a rainy day. An immovable vehicle parked by the side of the road was stuck and trapped in a big rut. It was a Nissan vehicle. A Nissan Pathfinder SUV. That was when I had a good lesson on Leadership from my Dad. May his good soul rest in perfect peace. I watched him speak passionately, read his lips as I listened attentively just as he would expect. It's a pathfinder, he said. It's supposed to have a helping gear. It cannot be trapped like that. Unless something else could be the reason. Pathfinder SUV cannot be immovable in the rut. After this experience, I became very curious. Not about cars but the name 'Pathfinder'. Growing up and choosing to researching and lecturing in strategic leadership principles, theories and practice, I encountered *Pathfinding* as a powerful word. If you are a pathfinder, you are a leader.

In the words of my dad, you cannot stop on your journey as a pathfinder. A pathfinder should be self-motivating. You pioneer and always ready to set the tone to flow forward as a trailblazer. Once upon a time in my office, there was a hanging on the wall in the open. Do not follow where the path may lead, go instead where there is no path and leave a trail -Ralph Waldo Emerson. In life, few people do new things. Don't be too excited to inherit success. It is beautiful to add on to success. Interestingly, it is satisfying to break new grounds. Be a pathfinder. Do not be trapped. Becoming a pathfinder is to see opportunities and going for them.

A pathfinder will define new grounds and drive through the rut (just as my dad expected). Pathfinders go with the blue ocean strategy and are not students of the red ocean. Pathfinders are always willing to learn from their teams. Pathfinders learn new things with a simple concept that 'if you don't start you don't finish'. The whole idea is to find the path. Finding the path is the solution to the main problem. People don't start yet they want to finish. Not starting also means doing all the work from conceptualization to preparation and shelving the idea in the end because of obstacles. Pathfinders go through obstacles (I didn't say traps). Pathfinders are alert and are always willing to try again even if they fail. They know that after all, no doesn't mean never. We all break down sometimes. That's human. Everybody hurts. But as long as we have room to bounce back, pathfinders must keep on pathfinding so others can follow. Leadership is about taking that giant, bold, question-asking and answer-finding steps to create a new path for others to follow to fix situations. Every transiting point in pathfinding comes with its own beautiful experience. If you want to be a Pathfinder never abandon any of the opportunities you meet along the way to wait for another. This is a secret. Build capacity and grab the opportunities. Find the path. Involve the team. Ask! If you have to. I've searched and researched everywhere for a befitting definition for a 21st century-leadership description and I have concluded that bold leadership is Pathfinding.

On a long expedition, you need direction to stay on track. When you find the path for the team, you chart the course. To chart a course is to lead, open and show the way. For me, one of the phrases in leadership that keeps me awake all day and all night is 'charting a course'. There are always impediments on the journey to leadership development. Unfortunately leaders cannot express weakness and cannot also fall for impediments along the way. If leaders don't exhibit the energy to clear the way, their followers won't have the motivation to see ahead, together.

A leader cannot keep his head down always. A leader must see the bigger picture. A leader must chart a course. A leader should set sail. A leader steers the team. A leader plans the path. A leader blazes the trail and the leader navigates the way. In a corporate training, a participant asked me, so what else shouldn't the leader do? He shouldn't be sleeping, I answered. Your purpose as a leader in the lives of your followers, is to create a path and chart the course to a defined destination. That destination must be known from the very beginning. The imaginary thought of a final destination whets the appetite for continuous preparation and constant calibration. A leader must always paint a picture of the journey to the followers. At least everyone deserves the chance to know how close or how far the ship will sail. Do not forget to measure the KPI's on the journey. Charting a course was initially a naval term where officers used charts to navigate their way. It relates to deciding which way to go. As a nautical term, to chart a course was more of plotting.

In one of my corporate trainings *'employeeitude'* I established that people need to chart a course either for themselves or their teams. To chart a course is to plot the journey to carry teams along. Every team has a story. There will be heartbeats when you attempt charting any kind of course especially if it's a new endeavour. Listen to the team. Listen to the beats. They send right signals. Intuition is crucial in leadership development too. In the book, Head, Heart and Guts (Dotlich et al 2005) it sums up a lot of good pointers. It is important to get a very good mix of everything including emotions, character, experience, knowledge and wisdom. When you find your direction, you don't dance with two left feet. To be pointy, identify your course. Focus. Act. Don't keep on talking. Paint the picture. Add more colours if you have to. Chart a course when you find the path. Go with the team. They are your helping gears. In leadership, also remember that, sometimes you have to go backward to move forward. If we understand pathfinding, we'll appreciate courage in leadership.

CHAPTER 13

Build the People

A good reward to a wrong recipient can collapse a good team

*****

There's always a step before the run. A strong foundation is needed for every good project. In other words, be sure of the foundation before you think of building. If you want to taste leadership, try building a team. A leader requires a greater motivation to build. Every builder has a dream just as leaders have. This is why leaders are builders. In building, it's regular to encounter pessimists, rejections, killjoys, fears, doubts, haters, society hoodlums, regulators, systems and sometimes yourself. Nonetheless, the pain, the anger, the neglect, the joy, the darkness, the laugh, the failures and the wins make a leader eager to keep on building. Good leaders build. If you are thinking of building, just start. Focus on the base. Fortify the corners. At the workplace, empower your supports and reports. Focus a lot more on people. It's always people, from day one. In my experience, when I started my company, I always say, people and others. It's pretty clear if you read and understood the chapter on laying the foundation. A onetime military dictator who became a democratically elected president of Ghana, Jerry John Rawlings, said 'Leadership should have confidence in our people and not feel intimidated by empowering them'. Leadership is not about power. It's mostly about empowerment.

In building, be open-minded and be ready to grow from a positional leader to an influential one. Form a team. Grow the team. Train the team to see the end of projects from beginning. It is very difficult but exciting as well. To select a team look out for people who have something to lose. People who have nothing to lose can easily give the vision away aside from not working towards it. Engage the team to challenge each other to drive the goals in support of the team's objectives. The challenge should be around improving competencies and expanding capacities. Leaders must communicate intentions clearly so that teams wouldn't think that dragging others down will elevate them. As a matter of fact, in building, leaders must communicate the motivation in delivering on tasks. Although a leader intends to get the team along, a leader would have to build strong alliances to influence teams. Let the standards be known and let it be measurable and be competed for. Standards must be known for total compliance. For example, every industry has its own regulatory requirements. Let the team know. Choose the right leaders to guide teams within the team. Don't fit the crown on the knee instead of the head. Reward. But do it respectfully with wisdom. Be objective, subjectively. Good rewards to wrong recipients collapse teams. Inasmuch as you activate strategies to keep a team motivated don't shake the table if you don't have to. Let the structure stand.

A structure within a team is like a fulcrum that directs systems and people within a space. So if a leader is tasked to build structures and to build people, he is as well tasked to link several parts of a body to survive shocks in line with an arranged plan. In effect, a leader is expected to connect and relate parts of something complex to function to meet a pattern as required by an organisation. When I say build the people, I'm saying that no good leader has accomplished anything remarkable alone. When you chart the course, as I hinted, you go with the people. At best, leaders develop succession plans to keep visions alive. Prepare today for future opportunities.

When you attempt to build structures to include the people, your test as a leader is to mould the team. Make the team strong. The strength of the wolf is in the pack. It's not an easy task to bring everyone up to speed. It is extremely crucial and a torrid scorching experience. To mould the team, place more emphasis on performance. If your focus is not on performance then there is no need wasting everybody's time. In moulding, your team will weigh your tolerance level and they will check your patience too. Obviously, they will check your expert power and they will investigate your passion.

Be deep as a leader. Tap into your gut and heart. Show your followers a lot more of courage in decision making and integrity in implementing policies, introducing processes, executing strategies, managing issues and handling challenges to demonstrate to them that you are human in showing interest in what they do and in developing their well-being at all times.

Leaders build and mould teams from ground zero and teams must be prepared to go through the stages. Tuckman makes it simple as summarized by Hughes et al (2015). Teams are formed to achieve a goal and within the same intention, to develop and to lead followers to reach their potential. In moulding teams, leaders must be conscious of this. Teams are often made up of people with diverse orientation, from education to work experience, from social backgrounds to age differences and from gender to different thinking abilities and patterns. Differences set enough tone for team friction. When teams are formed they storm. Every leader must anticipate this. Good leaders don't take sides. Good leaders are objective when team issues start springing up. Ahenkorah (2018) mentions that good leaders know that in teamwork there are issues and with teamwork there are no issues.

A leader should redirect team focus towards the goal, every time. This is where leaders introduce policies, standards, ethics and values to ensure that team norms well. And if a team is able to go through these phases, it is always easier for such a team to perform. When a team is performing, I describe that phase as 'no mountain is too high to climb and no river is too deep to swim in'. Here, everyone is ready to support each other to succeed. No one hurts. When a team performs over a long period of time, a leader must introduce mixed models of motivation to keep the team moving. When teams perform they adjourn. The adjourning stage can be controlled when the right motivation tool is applied. In moulding teams, Leaders must apply discipline fairly in dealing with team deviances. Fair discipline is to transfer an unwanted consequence or to remove a wanted consequence, with the likelihood that a certain conduct will not be repeated. In applying discipline fairly, a leader is correcting the unacceptable behaviour and not attacking individuals and personalities. The effective application of the leadership framework is the comprehensive discipline of the situation. Build people to mould a team.

CHAPTER

14

The Hot-Stove Rule Simplified

Good attitudes make good institutions

*****

I credit this chapter to the American Professor Douglas Murray McGregor who developed theories in Management in the late 1950s and early 1960s. He is the advocate of the hot-stove rule as a disciplinary tool at the workplace. He used an interesting analogy between the hot-stove and employees. When you mould the team, the next phase is to shape attitudes. Impose disciplinary actions with clear understanding of policies. Stimulating umbrages and unnecessary negative energies break teams. Good teams require adequate knowledge, skills and good application of the hot-stove theory.

I always use the hot-stove rule and it hasn't failed me yet. In my people management experience, I apply the hot-stove rule to shape attitudes and mind-sets. The hot-stove is a tool used to influence positive attitudes and discipline fairly negative behaviours at work. To avoid skirting around the main issues, the hot-stove rule brings clarity to leader motives. To be successful in using the hot-stove rule, employees must first know about it. You can choose to do a full orientation on it, so to communicate intentions with maximum respect and all seriousness. First, the stove is 'on fire', obviously it's hot. In other words, it will burn you when you touch it or you can feel the heat when you are getting close to the stove. The stove doesn't know any employee. It is just a stove. It's impersonal. Any disciplinary measure imposed should befit the weight of the offence and not the individual. The stove is not selective. It is worth noting that the stove is always hot and it thus burns immediately you touch it. You don't touch the hot-stove and feel the heat or hurt, later. Punishment and processes towards punishment shouldn't delay unnecessarily. To sum it up, the hot-stove is consistent each day, each time and to everyone who touches it. Punishment is super immediate.

The hot-stove rule simplifies disciplinary actions in good institutions. The only advice is that Human Resource Practitioners should not use this as a whip to destroy. It is a tool to build, to correct and to shape attitudes for workplace performance. I use it to inoculate cancerous teams because of the contagion effect in team building. Although good attitude is infectious, bad attitude is also pandemic. John C. Maxwell hinted that, good attitude may not guarantee success, but bad attitude surely guarantees failure. The hot-stove rule checks bad attitudes and stinking behaviours from spreading within teams. It is a good tool for effective feedback. To manage the contagion effect of attitudes, it is always crucial for leaders to tap into the broader understanding and the use of the hot-stove. I have had beautiful moments with the hot-stove rule. Anytime you tell your followers what you expect from them, tell them what you do not expect from them. Don't leave grey areas when establishing a culture at the workplace.

Manage team boundaries and manage team excesses. Cut every fat and stick to the flesh when dealing with disciplinary issues. If you don't let your team know what they are not at liberty to do, they will be at liberty to do everything because you didn't tell them. The whole idea about the hot- stove rule is to get the right fit. I liken discipline at the workplace to a rotten finger of banana amid a bunch of good bananas. If you kept the rotten one among the team, the good ones will be rotten in some few days. If you plucked the rotten one out, the good ones may stay longer even if they are not well preserved. Disciplinary decisions are choices. There is always a progressive line linking attitudes to a firm's performance. Good attitudes make good institutions. You can only get the team to focus on the corporate strategy when you shape their attitudes to connect to the organisation's mission. Remember, an institution is successful when it fully utilizes employees' potentials. It starts and ends with discipline.

CHAPTER

15

Let the Team Work

Even in the circus, clowns have objectives

*****

When you share your standpoint on discipline with the team, define the boundaries quickly. Guide the boundaries with policies or your '*laws*' if you like. As our learned friends will say, the law is the law and keep your structure in your policy enshrined within regulatory framework and the laws of the land. It's about ensuring that leaders do have grip to develop watertight policies aimed at encouraging the team to work effectively and efficiently. If an institution's policies, regulatory framework and the laws of the land are aligned, it's always easy to introduce reforms within your people strategy. The team should be kept together by the values of the company to enable leaders manage accountability and performance (Kaplan & Norton 2004). If they are not having common core values, teams can't deliver in line with leadership's expectation.

Every team has an objective. Leaders must focus teams towards a firm's objective daily. No team is put together to joke. Even in the circus, clowns have objectives. There will always be challenges in team development. The key is to ensure that the passion to build must be stronger than the forces and factors of team destruction. If you want the team to really come to work to work, tell them about your *Dos* and *Don'ts.* Be serious about this and remember, loose lips sink ships. Let the team value the institution's values by way of providing guidelines and standards towards your institution's culture. One thing I enjoy sharing with teams I manage is always about the *Dos* and *Don'ts* within any set up or space. The reason is simple. Two things always come up in people management. The team will do what you don't want them to do or they'll not do what you want them to do. Every leader goes through this. For leaders to manage these excesses, a leader must be authentic because followers will mirror leaders, eventually.

A leader must represent the value system of an institution because leaders represent culture of institutions. Dr. Amina Aitsi-Selmi said 'people don't leave jobs, they leave toxic work cultures'. In effect, people leave toxic leaders. If you want the team to work, show them the prize. In the Olympic Games for example, athletes know what is at stake even before they get into the tracks. If performance pays, let it be clear. If it doesn't, then the question is, what gets employees paid, promoted or elevated? A friend once joined a company where the CEO called him to his office one day and said to him, Jones! The only thing that would get you promoted is loyalty and not performance. He was straight to the point. So Jones asked for his definition of loyalty. He wished the CEO never explained to him. Because the more he did, the more he felt sorry to have joined that company. I can't explain further, because Steve Jobs summed it nicely that 'in weak companies politics win. In strong companies best ideas do'.

When the foundations are strong with clarity of purpose, institutions won't fail unless the uncontrollable happens. If you really want the team to work, introduce programmes and initiatives to let them work. If people come to work to work, work will always be fun because followers can measure their contribution and performance to the companies bottom-line. If you want to get more from the team, train them. As a CEO of a learning organisation, I've come to learn this. Training is an investment not a cost to the company. People ask, so what happens when you spend so much to train them and they leave? I don't think I have any answer. But every good CEO will answer with a question. What if I don't train them and they stay, quoting Zig Ziglar.

Letting the team work is about preparing the team, creating the right ambience for performance and growth, developing team competencies to subsequently empower them and more importantly trusting the team to grow. Within the trust, there must be controls.

For example, you trust the team to get to work on time which is why you have a timer to check employee attendance. Give them room to grow and delegate roles to check role growth potentials, learning gaps and motivational techniques. If you don't allow the team to work, you'll end up doing their chores. Remember, a leader hires employees to work so you can lead, guide and mentor. Don't be seen doing their work. Remember that you hired their brains. Let them use more of it! The 80:20 rule applies here too.

CHAPTER

16

Measure the Team

Life is boring without targets

*****

When you allow the team to work, measure them. It is always assumed that employees that make up a team might have gone through a team selection process. Team goals must be shared and team targets must be clear as always hinted. Never let teams get away with team targets. Each individual must be measured. Give each employee a SMART target. Hear this from me, life is boring without targets. Set targets for yourself and the teams you manage. To the point, enforce targets. When you live in this life without targets, you die early, because nothing challenges you to live to see another day. I prefer to use the SMARTER- Specific, Measurable, Attainable, Realistic, Time-bound, Evaluated, Readjusted- model. Everyone must be measured in a team and everything must be measured to get the team going. Honestly, there's no point keeping a team together without measuring their performance. For starters, leaders must select and keep employees with a cultural fit as well as persons who fit job roles. These are soft areas in selecting good employees. It is also crucial to team development.

Each employee is measured in a team because employees must sign contracts to agree to deliver on job roles. Welch (2005) advises that if you don't intend to put together a high performing team, why develop a team in the first place. So I'm always inspired and subsequently inclined to measure teams with standards that will push team limits and more importantly sustain institutional growth. My point is that, if you don't set standards, expect pig fights in the office if not loud dog barks. Inasmuch as a team's mission is crucial for team's success, it has become extremely fundamental for leaders to develop performance management systems, to ensure that every deliverable within the team structure is measured at the workplace.

As advised, performance management systems must be broken into perspectives so that leaders can measure everything including even the movements of the air in the office. In line with measuring a company's performance, Kaplan and Norton (2004) hinted four key perspectives for institutional leaders to note as they proposed the balanced scorecard, as far as measuring performance is concerned. They hinted that leaders should focus on financial, process, customer and employee perspectives. You can always replace employee perspective with employee learning and development or employee growth.

When you measure the team, reward achievers and sanction underperformers. I personally like to raise employees who exceed targets significantly. I do so because, I just don't measure the team, I seek to develop top (high) performing teams. I use the Rocket model (Hughes et al 2015) to develop top performing teams. The model sets a good tone to measuring ambitious teams. First, leaders must get the right Talent. I mean, get the followers who are ready to serve with apprenticeship mind-sets. Leaders must share team's mission in the morning, afternoon, evening and late at night (if they have to), so to get team buy-in. To ensure that teams stick to the corporate knitting, leaders must develop norms to shape teams. Beyond norms, leaders must whip up morale so to empower teams at all times. To conclude, it's always good to measure everyone. A good employee is the one that earns the leader's respect. Leaders must commit to ensuring that every member within the team has a target. Beyond the targets, leaders must introduce tried and tested performance management reviews and systems to manage team performance.

CHAPTER

17

The New Bold Leader-NBL

New bold leaders are objective and subjectively balanced. Strength is in the mind and not in the arms.

*****

The corporate world, in particular, is taking a new form where leaders continue to show the way. Leaders lead and teams follow, as always hinted. The workplace is witnessing times where hard work is not really paying anymore. Yet, employees who dance around and do others in, get the mentions. Pathetic. 21st century has thrown the challenge for the emergence of new bold leaders. A new bold leader won't reward employees for doing nothing. New bold leaders are objective and subjectively balanced. They reward employees when they exceed expectations. They don't reward employees when they meet expectations. New bold leaders reward just as they sanction to ensure that the equation would not be left imbalanced. New bold leaders reward and sanction employees to ensure that followers do not fall below expectations. They take decisions and stand by them. As a matter of fact, a new bold leader must hold on to some principles that would guide employee rewards, recognition, elevation and promotion as well as administering punishment. Although rewards and other recognitions and promotions are fused into work structures such that employees are promoted periodically for example, after performance management reviews (PMRs) in most institutions, the new bolder leader wouldn't have to wait for the end of PMRs to reward employees if they deserve admirations and commendations. The new bold leader wouldn't sit to be overwhelmed with challenges. They confront issues to curb the 'spread effect'. Just as in authentic leadership theory, the new bold leader lives the values and also live by the dictum 'to thine own self be true'. Every trait, behaviour, skill and even style is crucial for leader effectiveness and team success. The new bold leader knows this.

The new bold leader focuses on the prize and keeps the team stronger and closer to prepare them for dream assignments. As a leader, be not afraid to implement tough decisions that would benefit first, the institutions they lead and second, generations yet to come. New bold leaders are tactful in managing emotions and they keep an open mind to issues. They enjoy feedback and they don't hold on to positions. This is because they know that leadership is not about positions. Maxwell (2005), Ahenkorah (2018) and Hughes et al (2015) do not stop hammering that leadership is a process. New bold leaders don't live in positions. They leave positions to live in influence. New bold leaders learn, discover, groom, manage and stand up as martyrs ready to create successors for generational performance. New bold leaders incite team passion to build follower confidence. To keep the levers moving up and down there is always the need to whip up team enthusiasm to achieve team results. The new bold leader does this. There is always the need to link every team activity to the team's bottom-line. The new bold leader would look into measuring everything. This is because the NBL is self-aware, self- regulated and well alert to deal with situations in the VUCA world. Strength is in the mind and not in the arms. New bold leaders know this.

George (2010) asserts and I concur that leader authenticity is most crucial than the style, sometimes. To a would-be new bold leader, I can only ask you to STAND when the norm is to sit. It's not defiance. It's a new order. The norm is failing institutions. Stand for the right things with integrity.

CHAPTER

18

Spotlight and the Headlight

If life is the big stage the leader has to act

*****

Whether you are an effective or ineffective leader, your contribution to leadership will always bring you into the spotlight. This is the main reason why leaders always seek answers and not to create problems. As a matter of fact, every leader at some point would be asked why? And interestingly, all answers must provide solutions. Yes, I mean solutions. From my experience, I can always differentiate a good leading leader from a sleeping one. A leader who'll get things done will start by asking the right questions. So Confucius says that the man who moves a mountain begins by carrying away small stones. To the point, don't put yourself in the spotlight when you cannot lead. Otherwise you have to be in the spotlight even when you are failing. Let me share a 21st century leadership secret with you. If you are not prepared for the assignment, let it pass. You have to be prepared. Preparation is willingness plus capacity. If you have capacity and you are willing, then you are ready.

As a matter of fact, some leaders don't really care whether institutions fail or succeed. I call it irresponsibility in the highest order. The time has come in 21st century leadership where the spotlight has to be reserved for deserving leaders.

So what's the spotlight? Popular dictionaries will call it a lamp or even an uplighter that throws a powerful beam of light directly on to a person or even a place, especially a performer on a stage. Like they say, if life is the big stage the leader has to act. Anytime I think of a spotlight the legendary Michael Jackson comes to mind. The beauty of the spotlight is always about focus. When you are spotlighted, all you need to do is to show the crowd what you have. If you have nothing, just bounce. I mean leave. The point is, you have to do something. Everyone gets disappointed when you are under the spotlight and you offer nothing. To be promoted as a onetime high performing team member, you'll be tasked to deliver on specific objectives and if you fail miserably, the spotlight will still be on you. A true leader does not expose himself to be under this spotlight. The spotlight can be positive and it can also be negative.

The whole idea is that leaders must do something to earn their contracts; whether social or performance. When you are hired to perform on a big stage, just shine. When you miss out on the big stage and you get to be spotlighted in a street pub, still shine. One thing I learnt in leadership as far as the office is concerned, is to take my spotlight with me everywhere I go. I try not to let anyone dim my shine. In one of my speaking sessions, a brilliant participant asked me; how do I do that? Simple but tough, I answered. Stay in the spotlight. She asked again. So how do I do that? Once again I replied, simple but tough. Performance and consistency, I smiled. Staying in the positive spotlight is all about exceeding targets consistently. Don't rest on your paddles.

One other thing I noticed in leadership is that leadership has turned into showmanship echoing Zhang Weiwei. If we learn to appreciate what leadership is all about, we will clamour for consistency so to stay in the spotlight.

Sometimes good leaders get into positive spotlights and the back-end crews dim their shine. Actually, my favourites are those who get on stage and disappear with antics of the art of Houdini. To stay in the spotlight, leaders must learn to sustain the follower motivation to keep the back-end crew happy. Remember, the lights don't shine forever. You have to keep it shining. Serious countries create serious leaders. Same way, serious institutions create serious leaders. Serious institutions create many headlights. Headlight is a tool to equip people to see, essentially, in the dark. When you find yourself in the spotlight, you'll be seen and you'll always be short-changed if you don't see the people watching you. Obviously, it is not healthy to keep the equation imbalanced. Just to narrow what the headlight is, I would like to describe it as the powerful light at the front of a vehicle or even a bike. Yet, I would like to describe the headlight worn by miners who go on the underground and the powerful ones worn by the hunters who obviously go hunting.

The whole idea of the headlight is to provide vision. 21st century leaders know that they wear the headlight and without their lights on, followers wouldn't see ahead. An effective leader would need a headlight to show the way for followers to shine and do great things. Leaders with their headlights on, always know that they don't rule. They lead. You can never get lost when you have a vision. In very crucial terms, your vision is clearer with your headlight on. Your headlight is expected to make you stand out. So Ken Blanchard sums it that, leaders must work consistently and consciously to standout. Crowd may cloud your vision but focus on the headlight. The headlight principle is simple. Focus with the big picture in mind and keep achieving the operational deliverables towards the bigger goal.

Without the headlight principle in mind, you can't see far. Myopic leaders need to get their headlights on, to see farther. It's about direction, steering and seeing. Sometimes you don't need to do much as a leader. Just throw the light ahead for your team to see far. In effect, followers should be seeing their future through the rays of a leader's headlight. The headlight symbolizes a mantle of responsibility. Leaders who understand the headlight principle know that they don't rule but they lead. They show passion for what they do and also what they intend to unleash from followers. Passion ,here, is a combination of vision and feeling.

The headlight must provide strong vision and must generate adequate enthusiasm to keep the followers awake throughout the journey. Throw the headlight as far and fast as you can so to ensure that your vision is clear before you set off. The beauty is that, you can never get lost when your vision is clear. Keep it on when you find yourself in the woods. When you train to wear your headlights on, you work on your mind. It is very important to keep the mind working because if the mind fails to work, the body works in vain. Headlights provide warmth, comfort and enthusiasm to teams. If headlights become hazy, change it! Leaders must get their headlights working all the time and their lights must go ahead of them to secure the destination even before they get there. Followers are always ready to go the mile, unfortunately leaders are not providing the right motivation to urge them on. Office teams, like any other team, must demand that leaders show the way. When you find yourself in the spotlight, get your headlight on.

CHAPTER

19

The Plus One Attitude

If you want to see yourself rising,
you have to do more than more

*****

Leaders come, leaders go. Some come to stay and go nowhere. Some live in our minds and hearts generationally. Others spit venoms that break bones perpetually. Some leave behind wide and clear lenses for a whole community to see through. Some create collective compelling visions for everyone to see through to walk towards the finishing line with a clear picture in mind. Others destroy the structures laid down by their forerunners and may never contribute to building anything. The plus one dialogue goes beyond performance. It's about sacrifice, commitment, doing more and consistently going beyond great, stretching expectations.

I've worked under a leader with a plus one factor and I called him the plus one leader. I really relished the grooming. Honestly, I wouldn't trade that experience for anything. I was stretched (chortling as I write). Oh yes, I was. If you work under a plus one leader and you are ready to build a plus one attitude to stand out with a plus one factor, you'll always be ahead of competition or better still, you'll be ahead of yourself. You can only develop the plus one factor in the corporate world when you exceed management's expectation, contribute to other team's deliverables, commit to rise above self, peers, challenges and always learning to be ahead of workplace challenges. Remember, you are your own benchmark! There should also be the internal passion to keep doing better above expectation.

In 21st century leadership, leaders have no option than to rise above challenges and be willing to set straight unbending bars. To have a plus one factor, you go beyond targets and expectations. There is always a silent request to stand up for yourself and for the team's targets. If you work under plus one leaders, you'll be conscious of the plus one factor because a plus one leader creates plus one followers. A plus one leader doesn't just promote employees. They keep on asking key questions like, is Jane exceeding specific deliverables? And what extra factor has Jane got over Kofi? If the answers are not clear enough, Jane wouldn't be promoted ahead of Kofi.

In leadership, there is always a big difference between meeting and exceeding deliverables. So I led a session in Accra, Ghana, and a participant genuinely wanted to know why she's not been promoted after working in a firm for years and to her endless surprise, junior colleagues she inducted were climbing up the ladder and getting all the promotions, elevations, accolades and recognitions. My answer was simple. You need the plus one! So I asked; beyond your job description and performance (which I failed to query), what else are you bringing to the table? I mentioned to her that although I don't know the kind of leader she works with, the 21st century workplace is currently churning out new breed of plus one leaders who always demand more than specific job descriptions.

To bring this point to the table, I actually painted a stimulating picture that plus one leaders always want dessert on the side when they actually pay for the main course. A plus one leader looks out for the plus one factor to justify any promotion or elevation at the workplace. Employees who develop the plus one factor always have an edge over those who don't. As Welch (2005) hinted that you are hired to perform, Ahenkorah (2018) asserts that in leadership development you only put your best foot forward when you look after yourself and look after others. Plus one factor doesn't mean relegate your core function to develop other skills in other departments. The plus one factor requires you to perform significantly to exceed on core deliverables and to subsequently contribute to other functions in other departments. When you develop your plus one factor, you'll always be felt even when you are long gone. If you want to see yourself rising in leadership, you have to do more than more.

CHAPTER

20

Leadership Fatigue

April showers may not bring May flowers

*****

One of the challenges we find in leaders which is gradually becoming invidious to our ecosystem is leadership fatigue. Some would call it L-squared: Leadership Lassitude or Leadership Lethargy. The question which is incessantly difficult for leadership discourse is whether people get tired legs before they get into leadership positions or people get into leadership positions and develop weak legs. It is fine to get tired legs sometimes, but it is of great concern to have tired brains. It is sad when leaders don't get anything done. Yet, we keep them there as a decorative piece left to fill vacant ridiculed positions, but for a while. Imagine yourself as a passenger in a coach on a highway being driven by a fatigued sleeping driver who occasionally wakes up and looks around to check if others are watching.

This is not about a faulty bus. It's not about a wrong direction. It's also not about an empty fuel tank. This is about a fatigued leader. Hales, as far back as 1986 attempted to drum home what manager effectiveness is all about. In short, I quickly inferred that, testing leadership effectiveness is about checking what a leader does and what the leader is expected to do. The gap will obviously tell you who an effective leader is and who an ineffective leader is. If you have zero gap for a leader, then that leader should be getting the thumbs up. In effect, if you achieve 80% of your targets you are 20% ineffective. In the same vein, if you achieve 20% of your target, you are 80% ineffective. If the gap keeps widening by day, leaders would keep veering off the road. Remember the scenario, a sleeping leader on a highway would veer off the road and crash into anything and that would be the end of a whole team's dream. So the question is: why are they behind the wheels?

Sometimes someone 'puts' them there. In other cases, they work their way to the top and they get complacent and fatigue sets in, eventually. This happens when leaders see success as a destination. Those who get there without merit, time surely catches up with them. It has always been a matter of time. The big question is, for how long would they be there for? It is worth asking because leaders in this category, most of the time, don't get things done and sadly destroy what forerunners leave behind. They always believe that April showers will surely bring May flowers. In effect, they watch things to flow and they passively exit without causing any change to things because they've been sleeping through their time. For those who worked their way to the top and later got fatigued, followers must wake them up. It may not be their doing. My argument has always been that, there's nothing wrong if someone 'puts' you there. After all, what's wrong in tapping into networking? Yet everything is wrong, if you fail to earn your shirt when you are in the driving seat.

The easiest way to feel complete is when you become complacent about the things you do and even dangerously, the things you don't do. This is funny but true. Some leaders seriously get fatigued easily due to peer pressure. Oh yes, peer pressure! If leaders fail to keep awake, they lose track and their roles are not exciting anymore for would-be leaders to offer themselves for mentorship. Current places of work have been struggling with some breed of fatigued leaders who are interested in the position and not the process. A lot of them clamour for the goodies and freebies and not the duties, liabilities and accountabilities. Leadership is a skill developed overtime, I always echo. You do it, because you are ready. You don't get weary until you step aside.

CHAPTER

21

Lead-A-Ship

Foresee storms and turbulence. It's part of the beautiful journey

*****

Leadership as a subject, is always interesting to discuss. No matter how the subject is shared, people always have their opinions. As said, opinions are like noses. Some claim that people in authorities lose their memories and develop living signs of amnesia when they get into leadership positions. The argument has always been, where do the right thinking senses of leaders go to when they are needed for strategic thinking. For me, leadership (lead-a-ship) is to learn the skills to lead a ship. Whether you go ahead of the ship or you seek to steer the ship, you need this skill. In organisations, the leader groups a team to achieve a common goal. This should be noted. Maxwell (2015), Welch (2005), Armstrong (2004) and Ahenkorah (2018) will always remind readers. If leaders for example keep their team on a ship on a journey on the high seas, they have absolute responsibility to interpret the direction of the compass to their followers.

There are always instances and it is also normal for the crew to nap when ships sail, but not the leader. Call him a shipmaster, a captain, a sea captain, a ship's captain or even a master and he'll show you his worth. A ship's captain cannot sleep on duty. If he does, then what makes him the captain and where lies his duty? A shipmaster is supposed to be a licensed, highly qualified, legally and professionally approved high-level mariner who commands and holds ultimate responsibility of the ship's business. It's worth noting that the ship travels on oceans and deep waters which is why they are supposed to be large watercrafts requiring special skill to steer. They may come as oil tankers, bulk carriers or as container ships. The ship leader must be relational with high levels of expert and referent powers.

The leader requires the skill to keep the crew happy and the crew would in turn make the passengers happy and that would obviously make voyages exciting. Good lead-a-ship CEOs apply the theory of affectivity (Hughes et al 2015) in the offices, to raise happy teams. Shipmasters start their journeys with team briefs as well as inviting diverse opinions in a bid to grow team confidence. CEOs who learn from the ship Captain's approach to leadership development, listen to every member of the team, they are responsive to team requests as well as leading by example. Captains foresee perfect storms and beautiful turbulences in the spur of moments, thus they are always prepared for all kinds of eventualities.

Lead-a-ship style of leadership requires boldness to step in, step out and step up. Lead-a-ship styled leaders exhibit more self-control, self-regulation, listening and critical thinking skills with sound judgment in dealing with issues.

Leaders may struggle to lead teams and subsequently deal with issues, but if they learn to lead-a-ship, they'll surely be making great strides to understanding leadership from a lead-a-ship perspective.

CHAPTER 22

Tomorrow Today

Think tomorrow. Act today

*****

Leadership is a beautiful experience. The fact that it gives room for future thinking also creates opportunities for many fantasizers to lead teams, organisations and countries. What you think of today and subsequently say afterwards, must guide what you do tomorrow, in leadership. In other words, let your thoughts shape your speech so you can be circumspect in your actions. You just don't say what you cannot do, in Leadership. This is simply because a leader's right to perform on a job as a leader has been upheld as sacrosanct to the position being occupied. To the point, tomorrow owes no apology to the decisions you make today. Growing up as a boy I always admired a television programme, Tomorrow Today. For no reason I gained interest in the fact that tomorrow will be a better judge on the decisions we make today because tomorrow won't feel sorry for today.

In effect, I always looked forward to subsequent episodes. My simple understanding as a teen was that if you need a green environment, go clean and grow green. In leadership, you plan how you intend to live. My understanding has been, think tomorrow act today. But as you live to see tomorrow, you still have the opportunity to see another today, tomorrow. Don't waste today to secure tomorrow. Tomorrow today should remind leaders not to eat the seed but to wait for the fruits. Yew (2000), shared some lessons and legacy of a Leader. His book, From Third World to First World, The Singapore Story: 1965-2000 brings out the charisma of a leader who sees tomorrow, prepares for it and was thus never afraid to act today for tomorrow's generation. Even though the book captions some of the refreshing leadership style of Lee Kuan Yew, Milne (2000) also summarised the pro-activeness of Dr. Kwame Nkrumah when he sought to act for tomorrow's generations.

Tomorrow today brings reality to situations and it also provides a platform to deal with situations before they get out of hand. Having a Tomorrow Today mind-set prepares leaders to fly freely in their minds to a situational destination. Many problems are our own creation. Hence, we need to put minds together to create a better tomorrow. Don't kill genuine minds. Bring good minds together. Mend them even when they break. Leaders who build a tomorrow today approach to leadership development, go with smart brains. Followers must not have the best brain in the room. Great leaders who believe in tomorrow today, need followers with potential. Today may require the best of brains but tomorrow will always call for people with potential. Today's best may be obsolete tomorrow. As leaders look into the future (that's if they really do), today keeps staring in their faces. If today is good, tomorrow must be better. Life must be progressive and so must leadership decisions. To sum it all up. David Nicholls says and I quote: 'This is where it all begins. Everything starts here, today'

CHAPTER

23

Blink

Learn to control blabbing so to increase action

*****

I like leadership. I admire leaders. I always want to know the things they do and what they don't do. When followers make demands and subsequently push the walls consistently and persistently, one thing may happen out of the two. You see an effective leader or you'll see an ineffective leader.

When followers stay awake, leaders must not sleep. When followers sleep, leaders can only blink. Leadership requires that decisions are made within a blink of a moment especially in this fast-paced cunning rickety environment. To the point, leadership is about commitment, 360 degrees. A leader must be serious and steady- going at all times. New leaders must also learn the art of blinking by taking decisions on their feet. This requires adequate doses of intelligence. Hughes et al (2015) and Ahenkorah (2018) confirm that 21st century leaders must be intelligent analytically, practically, creatively and emotionally. Intelligent leaders master the blink. In difficult times, good leaders go with the blink. In crisis, good leaders show up.

Leaders stand out to create good conditions for followers and not to scream in the rain in tears and fears. Leaders control blabbing to increase action. Learning to stand when everything is falling requires a beautiful skill of blinking. When you go into yourself and you come out, the process takes the mind on a beautiful journey from home. In recruitment interviews for example, a good leader, without interacting with applicants, could tell who should be in or out. Although the leader cannot always be right in this context, a leader with the right skill of blinking, wouldn't be far from right either. Leaders who practice the blink have a way of taking people on quick mind trips.

The blink is a skill developed over time to form part of leader instincts. Leaders struggle in their roles if they fail to develop this skill. It is inbred and the challenge is that, leaders may not know when this skill may be required. It's like thinking on your feet. It's also about having good intuition. The lack of the art of blinking makes leaders wobble dangerously under pressure. If the world is believed to be in constant crisis, then the world needs leaders with cool heads. Hence, leadership must provide constant direction. Here, leaders must not give in to pressure. Their inherent aptitude must provide relative amount of calmness needed to control self, people and situations. Which is why leadership proposes that leaders operate in unruffled spaces with the mastery of the blink. This makes the art of the blink very crucial for leadership discourse. How do you remain calm, do and make quick decisions in a VUCA world? To do or not to do is insistence on the situation. Quick decisions in crisis must provide solutions, quickly. To assert your dominance is in your T-pose. The T-pose is to stand straight and stretch both arms to the left and to the right. This empowers you to appreciate the reality and the abstract responsibilities to control your area.

When you blink, literally, the eyelids tend to spread a cocktail of mucous and some amounts of oils secreted on the surface of the eye globes just to prevent the eye orbs from drying out. Learning to make decisions within a blink helps leaders to clear substantial amount of stress from work schedules and subsequently makes leaders see clearly. Leaders who learn the leadership art of blinking are decisive. They think fast. They think smart. Leadership is always going through some kind of scrutiny because of its monstrous, elusive, snow-balling and enigmatic nature as always hinted. If leaders intend to wait for a perfect moment to act, leadership would never happen because there's no perfect picture. Blink to capture the moments. Blink to decide on the go. Blink to learn to make decisions in seconds. Blink to tap into your instincts. Blink to see from a distance. Blink to live in the future. Blink to keep the dream alive. Leaders who learn the art of blinking gets there before the reality arrives.

CHAPTER

24

Blind Spots

Delegate. Don't abdicate

*****

Leadership puts leaders to series of erratic tests from situation to situation. It presents reasoning to leaders and subject leaders to reason on the go. Yet leadership is not all about reasoning. It is also an art which will always demand mastery of emotional management and intelligence, passion and inspiration (Thomas 2006). This makes leadership ever demanding. So I heard a failed leader screamed, Leadership is crazy! I curiously asked, why? How come a leader did nothing wrong and still failed, he answers. Then I shared the concept of the blind spot with him. Leaders don't see everything coming. When leaders gain mastery to know and feel that leadership naturally involves the interaction of the leader, the follower and the situation, they learn to appreciate that leadership is not about the leader.

This is the main reason why leaders need to adopt varying skills in leading teams to become adaptable to the ever-changing situation. Now let's get down to it. I don't want to be the stoolpigeon, but the fact must be established that leaders don't see every situation in the leadership space. Good leaders with great leadership skills see more through people. As a matter of fact, Hughes et al (2015) mention that leadership is about working through people to get results by organizing, coordinating and directing teams to behave in an expected manner. To the point, leaders have blind spots but that shouldn't lead to chronic incompetence.

Blind spots in leadership are areas leaders cannot see or they are areas leaders cannot see clearly probably due to physical obstruction or otherwise. For example, in managing geographically dispersed teams (GDTs), leaders must adopt relevant skills to get results. Activities of GDTs will always be at the leaders blind spot. Here, leaders must use mixed approaches as delegation, internal reporting systems, technology, performance management reviews and team empowerment programmes as powerful tools. Leaders must be reminded not to delegate to modern day politicians clad in corporate looks in the offices who will be fanning egos. Delegate to employees who will get the job done. Delegate. Don't abdicate (Ahenkorah 2018).

A leader's thinking pattern is affected if he has a lot of blind spots to manage. If leaders fail to deliberately identify blind spots so to deal with them appropriately as they come, they will do a lot of guess work and their directions and decisions will be flawed with speculations. Learn to use the blink. Learn to shut and open the eyes. The only challenge in fixing the blind spot with the blink, is about timing. Some leaders shut when they have to open and others open when they have to shut. If followers intend to take advantage of your blind spots, confront the team and be assertive about matters. Don't be aggressive. Visit and do road shows if teams are geographically dispersed. Don't enjoy sitting in the comfort of your offices. Keep yourself awake. If you start experiencing signs of vision impairment, get your glasses on. A leader must see. Remember that the leader is always the vision bearer. Never lose that status whatsoever. Yes. Leaders would have blind spots. If leaders use the right management tools in the right proportion, every area under management will be subordinated to leadership planning, management, organization and control. Leaders must learn to be continuously abreast of current trends whiles building capacities to remain relevant at all times.

CHAPTER

25

Lost Leaders

If a leader cannot be felt then the leader probably cannot be found

*****

It sounds good when leadership authors, speakers and trainers write and talk about what leadership is and often times remain silent on what leadership is not. Painting the picture for leadership mentees and trainees to walk into the role throws the whole concept of experiencing leadership into a frail grail of grey. To look to the left or to the right starts the process of leaders getting lost before they start the journey. Positively tamed aggression or assertiveness (if you like) and passion are the least of ingredients required for leader success.

Every good, performing and progressive leader wouldn't stop learning (Barnes 2005). Hughes et al (2015) quoted JFK the 35th President of the USA, that, 'leadership and learning are indispensable to each other' as already hinted. There are many lost leaders at the workplaces and high offices. They are present in their posts but are absent in their deeds. Leadership must be felt. If you cannot feel your leader then you probably cannot find your leader. Aside from the fact that sometimes you may not feel your leaders, it's even more dangerous when you cannot find them. They may be lost. Yes, lost! Leaders get lost in themselves on their journeys. It's fine if it's episodic. It's a nightmare if it's chronic. A lost leader remains weary without results, on a long journey. It is always the responsibility of every leader to bond well with teams to build confident, supportive, result- oriented, forward looking and ever prepared teams. We all need each other. Leaders must do a lot more of self-talking, self-introspection and self- awareness tests on yearly, half-yearly, quarterly, monthly, weekly and on a daily basis so to stay on track and subsequently map out a safe path through the woods so to get to the desired leadership destination. Leaders who learn the leadership art of blinking don't get lost, anyway. They think on their feet and are decisive on their journeys. They don't get lost because they are always ahead of the journey before they start. A colleague once worked under a lost leader. The leader was always lost in translation and in negotiation. One dominant thing was the fact that he sees within his box. He was always lost outside his walls.

From my experience, I shared with the colleague that lost leaders invariably exhibit traits of selfishness and greed. Leadership is always going through some kind of scrutiny because of its snow-balling, enigmatic and ever-changing nature (Munroe 2005) as already hinted. Thus, if leaders intend to wait for a beautiful moment to act, it would never happen. Don't get lost to miss the moments. Leaders who stray cannot take relevant decisions. Followers wield power from teams when leaders go astray. Over the years, it has come to dawn on me that followers do not necessarily go after power or wrestle for power with or from leaders. Leaders rather give power and influence away if they go astray. Leaders must learn to read the map to understand the mappings. True leaders don't tell people who they are. They show them who they really are. As always hinted, don't say it. Do it! Don't get lost. Be the bar. Set the pace. If you have to be intuitive, be! See the journey from a distance and guide your every step. On a journey of a hundred steps, the first step is as important as the hundredth step as well as the second, the fiftieth and the ninety-ninth. In short, every step is important on the journey not to be a lost leader. Walk into the future. Be on the path to keep the dream alive. Don't get lost in your steps.

CHAPTER

26

Remove Shoulder Pads. Burn Knee Pads

Don't fight to win. Not all fighters are winners. Not all winners are fighters

*****

In 2017, I facilitated a leadership workshop and networking seminar at Cape Coast in the Central Region, Ghana. Two interesting issues came up. Number one: why and how do most leaders become 'dictators'? Number two: why do most leaders cringe when situations require bold decisions?

I must confess. I really had a good time answering both questions because I achieved my three major objectives during the session. We learned. We unlearned. We re-learned. In my response, I shared with the participants that *"If you put on a blindfold and threw a dart at a map of the world, there is a 70 percent chance that whatever country the dart lands on is run by some form of dictatorship." RT Hogan, Hogan Assessment Systems (Hughes et al 2015 p.615).* True democracy is a fighting word (Crick 2002) and leaders are not ready for the *'fight'*.

Democracy reduces a leader's utmost *'power'* though it doesn't take away a leader's authority and responsibility. Most leaders find it difficult to share power. In the leader-member exchange theory (Armstrong 2004), leaders are expected to learn how to share power in the area of decision making in particular and how teams are managed in general. It's a skill to allow teams to make input into leadership decisions. In organizations, good leaders can solicit for teams input through team meetings, team briefs, staff durbars, management roadshows and even random team hangouts and staff mixers.

Leaders who come down to the level of their teams, see things differently and they see no point to wield power unnecessarily. The time has come in leadership discussions where the leader must learn to be modest and remove all shoulder pads so to relate well with teams. This is why understanding referent power is a crucial skill in leading teams, in 21st century leadership. Good leaders don't just listen. They listen. They listen very well and they listen to the end. During the same session, other participants were waiting gently, patiently and earnestly for a good answer on the second question. I told them brusquely!

Most leaders put themselves in many conflict of interest situations and they find it difficult to deal with crunch matters. No man in his right senses would want to deliberately and willingly exchange his eye for a toe. Leaders must learn to be well-founded. There's no point to be an aggressive leader. There's no delight to be an acquiescent leader. 21st century leadership demands firm and bold leaders. Don't fight to win. Not all fighters are winners. Not all winners are fighters. Good leaders don't apologise for making good decisions. Don't live in fear. Don't go begging to be accepted. Burn the knee pads. Don't be apologetic to bold decisions. Stand upright and get things done rightly. Be positive. Practice positive affirmation and don't stop improving yourself. Leaders must pursue knowledge in this 21st century knowledge-based world. If the rebels say power isn't given but it's taken, so is knowledge. Don't leave yourself behind. Attend workshops, seminars, read new books, try new things, share new knowledge, do further studies, listen to audio books, get knowledge and don't stop learning, re-learning and unlearning. Do well to know more, have foresight and practice knowledge gained. When you get the knowledge, apply meaning to it. That is wisdom. When leaders learn to appreciate people by learning to understand the world from a good perspective, they'll surely remove the shoulder pads and they will certainly burn the knee pads. Humility, confidence, wisdom and fearlessness are powerful to leadership development. Remove shoulder pads. Burn knee pads!

CHAPTER

27

Leader Nemesis

If you don't deliver on what you say, your nemesis will lead you to fail

*****

It's galling when leaders sham as though they know yet they know not. The words leaders say heighten follower emotions consciously, subconsciously and unconsciously any day, anytime. The major leader nemesis is what the leader says. The inescapable agent that would surely come after a leader would remain a leader's promise. The words of leaders should give hope, guide and shape teams. But when words fail to inspire but rather disappoint, leaders pay for empty promises. It's always said in various forms and shapes that you cannot reap what you haven't sown. Leaders can get away with everything but not with what they say. If you sing, be prepared to dance to your tune. In my country, Ghana, there's a funny street phrase which advises that '*if you cannot spell it, don't write it*'. Simple! If we dastardly deceive the people consciously to promise excessively so to get follower buy-in, we should be prepared to be answerable to their excessive demands palpably.

What leaders forget is that those promises arm followers to fight back and bite harder when they are ready to. I learned the rudiments in managing information especially when leading a large team at the workplace. You don't give information. You manage information. Don't give TMI (Too Much Information) away. In team dynamics, leaders are tempted to give TMI to wield unnecessary power. Even though what leaders say or may not say could be used against them in future, it's a difficult situation when leaders need to justify what they actually say or did not say. Leadership journey paves the way and subsequently gives room to leader scrutiny. Napoleon Hill puts it nicely, *'think twice before you speak because your words and influence will plant the seed of either success or failure in the mind of another'*.

In leadership, whatever you say is inescapable. Men die. Vision doesn't. Leaders with good intentions share their objectives to obtain follower buy-in. Good vision must have succession. Inspired by Dr. Myles Munroe, true visionaries create successors and a good vision must be handed down generationally. If what leaders say appears to be clear without ambiguity, followers will follow without hesitation. But if what leaders say turns out to be a con then they must be coerced to kiss the frog. Painting a compelling vision is not about making promises to your teams. It's about eagle-eyeing the end from the starting point and actually walking towards the vision and measuring the walk step by step with your eye on your steps and creating footprints to guide the steps. To avoid failure, some leaders make hard decisions not to share their vision but rather focus on getting the job done. This may sound beautiful but it's not inspiring enough.

A picture may say a thousand words, but it is better to walk your team into the vision. Share the vision. If leaders share their vision, followers become innovative and they tap into their inner strengths to work for and with the leader to ensure words become works. A whole lot of things run through a leader's mind. Words are leaders' nemesis. Good leaders guide their tongues. Your tongue may take you there and the same tongue may bring you back. You can't escape your words. It is the leader's nemesis. As long as leaders cannot stop talking, leaders shouldn't stop walking. As it is always said, *leaders should walk the talk.* If you don't deliver on what you say, your nemesis will lead you to fail. Ahenkorah (2018) hinted that *words are powerful.* Integrity, honesty and being true to one's own capacity and competencies are extremely crucial to leader nemesis. Leaders must occasionally weigh themselves by conducting self-audits. There is an African adage that advised that when you enter into a village and you see everyone and the village folks '*moving*' on their heads down with their legs in the air, '*move*' in the same manner before you ask why. Learning to understand your environment is a skill. One thing I observed in leadership is that every good leader must have the MICS. A good leader must have good Morals. A good leader must have Integrity. A good leader must be Competent. Finally, a good leader must be Sincere. In effect, morals, integrity, competency and sincerity are crucial ingredients for leader success. Be mindful of whatever you say and whatever you do or it may be your nemesis.

CHAPTER

28

Leader Dilemma

One good decision today may not be the best of decisions tomorrow

*****

Leaders go through daily challenges in making decisions. Some dread the process. To look to the left or to the right, plants leaders in dilemma. One big worry for leaders is the fact that one good decision today may not be the best of many decisions tomorrow. This is a fact.

Heraclitus said 'no man ever steps in the same river twice, for it's not the same river and he's not the same man'. Leaders go through self-experiences and every experience is a lesson. This is the main reason some leaders dawdle to decide. Yes, it is good to be a quick thinker. Yet, it's prudent to be meticulous somewhat slow and getting decisions right. It is logic to make good decisions out of bad options. Like morality, choosing between right and wrong shouldn't be a difficult process. This is obviously a no brainer.

Leaders would rather have challenges with dilemma situations where they have to choose between two 'rights'. Most of the time, decisions compete and leaders have to decide anyway. Sometimes values and priorities contest a leader's time and resources. What makes the decision process difficult is the fact that the entire team would be watching keenly and this heightens the degree of dilemma in making one decision. Making the right decision between two rights is also about leader ethics and principles and not necessarily about priorities. Kidder, in Hughes et al (2015) acknowledged four shared ethical dilemmas: Truth versus loyalty, Individual versus community, Short-term versus long-term and Justice versus mercy.

A good leader may be inclined to please the employer at the expense of the institution. The truth would be that, the institution may be struggling. But in the name of loyalty, and because some leaders would be willing to sell their conscience, they find themselves in a dilemma. Leaders sometimes focus on themselves at the expense of an entire team. Some also forget about long term needs and deliberately focus on short term goals and there are instances where leaders overlook wrongdoings to breed cancerous teams for organisations. In all these, Kidder once again offered three approaches to deal with ethical dilemmas when they come up (Hughes et al 2015). Use the ends- based thinking, rule-based thinking or the care-based thinking depending on the situation, to fix dilemma issues. With the ends-based approach leaders should focus on decisions that would be best for the majority of people. Some call it the utilitarianism principle.

The care-based approach is purely common-sense. The Holy Scriptures and popular religions preach always. 'Do what you want others to do to you'. The final approach is the rule based thinking which proposes that when leaders are in dilemma they should consult the highest principle or policy. I use this often times in people management. My big question to offenders has always been; what does policy say? It has been argued that you don't get innovative if you refer many times to policies. But I can also confirm that leaders who refer to policies in dilemma situations have come out champs even in adversarial conditions. Notwithstanding, note that beyond the policy, is the leader judgement. The policies and procedures must be respected within the context of the situation and using your sense of judgement to interpret and apply every word of the policy redefines objectivity in leadership dimensions. A leader shouldn't apply the rigidity of the policy but should be interested in the flexibility of the rules. It's not what the policies say but it is how the policy is applied and what it is used for.

Put your thinking caps on, when you find yourself in a dilemma situation. Remember, all the approaches proffered by Kidder in dealing with dilemmas require thinking. To manage dilemmas, a leader must be principled ethically and should be all-time ready to face surprises. What may be a dilemma today could be just an issue of morality tomorrow. Take your time. Decide right.

Choose right to win in dilemma situations. It's always about understanding the chapters.

A day shall pass. Another day will come. A day at a time may sound pleasing to the ear. Until we actually read to understand the chapters, we'll still be here. Understanding the activities of each day requires a lot more. A day in the life of a leader may be filled with stories, interesting scenes, songs, family matters, work gossips and sometimes avoidable dramas. Yet, leaders survive each day with pride so to start another day in humility and freshness.

Leaders go through phases as chapters of rough edgy storms pieced together by day. If you've heard anywhere that leaders learn on the go, it means leaders learn to understand the chapters as they unfold in their busy schedules. As long as leadership is also about finding solutions and enduring to deal with complex matters and inspiring multitudes, leaders have full obligation to understand the chapters to be prepared all the time. When you understand the chapters, you'll know when and how to flip the pages.

Leader preparation is not a pleasant process. It feeds into leader rites of passage, if you like. You stash more experience and shelve immaturity to understand the chapters as days go by. Every chapter must give a new learning experience. That's the whole idea. Not all leaders go through the process. Not all leaders read the chapters. That is why leader experiences are different. Some leaders flip the chapters in the process instead of reading. They don't go through the details.

It is known that some do corporate politics to get to the top and they get exposed in the end. The best way to do corporate politics is not doing politics at the office. Work your way up! Be seen and known as the employee who excelled to the top. That's glory. People who work their way up don't wade in credit taking. They earn team respect by taking on team responsibilities. It's one thing reading the chapters and another thing understanding the chapters. Don't be quick to run jumping up and down brushing through the chapters. Don't avoid sensitive issues affecting the team within the chapters.

Don't rubbish delicate team requests. Don't start discussions by ignoring the subject when issues are sensitive (Menkes 2006). Pick the signals. Weigh the team's emotional plight. Connect with team's emotions and show empathy, humanly. Don't justify actions with emotions. Be rational. Leaders who take time to read chapters word after word, acquire knowledge on knowledge. Once you learn to move ahead you look forward to the finish line. True leaders understand and share their life chapters with pride. Galileo said that' you cannot teach a person something he does not already know; you can only bring what he does know to his awareness'. True leaders easily identify with cultures. They are quick to know the philosophies that bond teams to achieve results. Understanding chapters refreshes the things you already know. Learn credible lessons from plans that didn't work and look forward to plans that are about to work. This should be the natural mind-set of a leader. Although you learn from the chapters of life in leadership in specific situations, every single chapter must add to the collective.

CHAPTER

29

Let the Team Fly

Don't throw a kite down from the top of a building. It will fly higher.

*****

It's a leader's responsibility to create leaders (Maxwell 1995).

Sometimes I shudder to understand why leaders develop leaders and subsequently become obstacles on the paths of mentees. Like my training manager once told me. Sir! If I work under you and get trained as a knowledge transfer professional, would you expect me to be a nurse or a knowledge transfer coach? Good followers look beyond a leader's achievement, which is why good followers should be better than leaders. Let the team fly. Don't take their shine. Don't suppress them. Give them power. I mean, empower them. For power is just a visitor. It doesn't stay. It may be with you overnight and may decide to stay longer with others. Sadly, power leaves you when you need it most. This is the more reason leaders must learn to give power away and rather crave for influence. Power is transient. In any case, use power wisely when you have it, because today it will be here, tomorrow it will be gone. It's like life. When you groom teams, bless them when they intend to leave. Yours is to fulfil your part as a leader (Menkes 2006).

Let your followers aim high. There is no traffic in the sky. The sky is too big enough for everyone. Don't suffocate team growth. Leaders form teams and groom them to adjourn. You don't subjugate teams. You grow them and exalt them to shine. Invariably, be the wings that support teams to fly. In my experience in building teams I found three categories of people in teamwork. They are the team members, the team players and the team owners. Team members are there for the team. Teams can function effectively without them. Interestingly, they possess all the traits of team players, yet they don't play for the team. They are passive. Team players are there for the team. They play their parts and go further to ensure that interconnectedness of team roles is fulfilled. They are always ready to help and they always see the success of teams as theirs. They are active within the team.

The third category of people, in my people development experience, is team owners. I always urge followers who dream to lead someday to aspire to be team owners. They inspire teams. They substitute their reputation for the team. They are quick to be there for the team and they are ready to groom their kind. They believe that power is not only transient but power is in transit to the next man. They aspire to inspire mates. Team owners are the new bold leaders who are ready to make other colleagues fly. They correct the team and make themselves small for the team to shine. They are selfless and they know that you don't train people and subsequently prevent them from flying. They actually own the woes of teams. They carry the blame and bounce the credit to the teams. If you want to grow a team from good to great, develop team members to become team owners. It's my little but top secret. If you grow team members to become team owners, you can always delegate tasks so to free your hands to do other things as a team leader. This is why I sometimes lark at leaders who take followers to the top and later wish they fall. It doesn't happen like that. Don't throw a kite down from the top of a building. It will fly higher. If you take teams up, let them fly. You'll surely be mentioned someday.

CHAPTER 30

Speak don't Skip. Be You

Don't tow the easy road that tells you that difficult matters require special moments to discuss

*****

It's always somewhat difficult to speak to the things that make or break. In Leadership development, learn to say it if it has to be said. Don't run from shadows. I mean, speak it. Don't skip it. What must be said can only be said. The skill to develop in speaking, however, is not only about what should be said. It is also about how it should be said. I often times hear that silence is golden. I respect that. But I don't raise cubs to become ducks. Some leaders are just acquiescent, and in an attempt to look 'good' in everyone's books, they lose their grip.

Leaders go leaders come as always said. But a leader must lead and speak if it so requires. Don't skip it. There are genuine reasons why a leader may pause and not speak. It doesn't also mean the leader shouldn't speak if he should. A leader must speak well. Develop the art of speaking. Hall (2007) advises that, there is no need to lose your confidence if you cannot speak well because there are ways to develop speaking coherently, clearly and concisely. Learning to speak and managing when to speak require certain levels of skill. When issues crop up at the office and within teams, don't let them grow uncontrollably. Speak. Don't tow the easy road that tells you that difficult matters require special moments to discuss. That moment may never come.

Good leaders start the process slowly in dealing with sensitive matters if they have to be discussed. Jim Rohn said 'if you really want to do something, you'll find a way. If you don't, you'll find an excuse'. There are always reasons why some matters are labelled untouchable. Speak! Don't be loud and don't be seen arguing. Be straight to the point, no excesses and be firm. I have handled corporate trainings on monitoring inner dialogues and I am firmly deeply rooted in my observation that every leader needs this skill. Beyond just talking to yourself, it is always crucial to anticipate reactions and refutations when managing team conflicts, for example. Some people may not want to go through self-communication reforms.

I learnt that I don't have to be always right. So when I speak, I create room for feedback. If other contributions are better than mine, I learn to connect my submissions to theirs to synergize ideas as well as learning to disconnect my ideas if it would negatively disrupt better contributions. I also learned to tarry my inputs if I had to. Learning not to skip but to speak is crucial in conducting meetings and in giving clear direction to teams. Leaders must gather the courage to correct followers if they have to. Speak, if you have to. Manage the emotions around situations and deal with it if it must be dealt with. Speaking and not skipping is about controlling your thoughts and expressing the things that ought to be said in a very polite, succinct and confident manner. Be quick to know what must be said and what should wait. Own your words and keep them close to your chest. Control when to reproduce it if you have to.

Sometimes all you have to do is to be you. Being you is difficult because situations always interfere with the self. It is fine to blend in. It is beautiful to tow the path of great men. Honestly, it is awesome to be who you have to be. Speak if you have to. Don't live in the horizon waiting for a beautiful day to appear. There's nothing like a beautiful day until you create it. Sometimes I get confused with some of the sayings from Confucius, but there's one that keeps me going. I quote, 'it doesn't matter how slowly you go as long as you do not stop'. I do not try looking around watching what others may be doing. Of course I'm mindful of competitor actions but I'm also happy about my action plans when they appear workable. It is all about direction and focus. Develop that attitude. In effect, keep going as long as you are on track. As hinted, focus means saying no to a thousand good ideas.

Don't get overly excited over nothing. You hold the keys to be happy or sad.

Just be you! There is one thing I discovered that built my confidence towards leadership development. Avolio (2010) hinted that leader development may occur in moments. They don't occur in minutes, days or weeks. Live in the moments and develop in the flashes. George (2010) nonetheless believes that individuals can develop authenticity if they are aware of their strength and internal weaknesses. If you fail to be you, there is the possibility of losing self-awareness as far as leadership development is concerned. It is good to look after people and teams but it is wise to be you when 'you do you'. You do not have to necessarily get it right to be you. Sometimes jump in and be yourself. The spokes may bend at you but when you learn to be you, everything smiles back. It is fine if life keeps you swinging from one pole to the other.

If you learn to be you, you will definitely find your sweet spot to map a path. When people yell at you, just take the positives and bin the negatives while you learn not to repeat same mistakes. Sometimes you need people who love you to remind you of what you should be doing for yourself. It is not wrong. Someone must keep you awake. When you learn to be you, you learn to do things and understand the patterns of life. When George (2010) proposed the five heights of authentic leadership to include values, relationships, heart, self-discipline and passion, he was pointing to one thing. If you want to be an authentic leader, do it yourself. Values are personal. Developing passion and self-discipline are self-decisions. It is good to have mentors but let them shape you to be you. Just allow your personality to grow and experience the process. When you learn to appreciate the OCEAN model on personality types depending on your viewpoint, learning curve, personal development and life experiences, I can only conclude that there is always strength in any of the personality types. When you learn to be you, you will always develop your personality type to lead. This book should open your eyes to see leadership differently. Yes! You need the team. First, build your influence and take the lead for the team to follow. Remember! The Leader. The Follower. The situation. This is Leadership!

This book seeks to heighten the Leadership Dialogue, every time.

Thank you for reading this book. Are you a good Leader?

Notes

Ankrah, J.K., 2014. Managing the pressure of success and time, Bridge of Hope

Ahenkorah, R.K. 2023 Your Journey to the Top (Revised Edition), BlueRose Publishers

Barnes, J.A., 2006, The lessons and legacy of a president: John F. Kennedy on Leadership, Amacom

Blanchard. K., Johnson, S. 2003: The one-minute manager Harper Collins

Collins, J., 2001. Good To Great, HarperCollins Publishers

Collins, J., Porras J.I., 2005 Built To Last, Random House Business Books

Covey, S., 1998: The 7 habits of highly effective people, Touchstone books

Covey, S., 2004: The 8th habit: from effectiveness to greatness, Free press

Dotlich, D.L., Cairo, P.C & Rhinesmith, S.H, 2006., Head, Heart & Guts Evans, V., 2018. Strategy Plain and Simple, Pearson

Hughes, R., Ginnett, R.C., Curphy, G.J, 2015 8th Edn Leadership: Enhancing the lessons of Experience McGraw- Hill Education

Goleman, D., Boyatzis, R., Mckee A., 2002. Primal Leadership, Harvard Business School Press

Harvard Business Review, 2011., On Leadership Harvard Business School Press

HBRP, 2017, Emotional Intelligence., Harvard Business Review Press

HBR's 10 Must Reads, On Leadership, 2011., Harvard Business Review Press

Hindle, T. 1998. Manage Your Time, Dorling Kindersley Limited

Jakes, T.D., 2017, Soar, Hatchette Book Group

Kaplan, R.S., Norton, D., 2004 Strategy Maps, Harvard Business Review

Kaplan, R.S., Norton, D.P., 2008, The Execution Premiûm, Harvard Business School Publishing Corporation

Keith, H., 2005. Attitude is Everything, HarperCollins Publishers
Korn F., 2014-2015. FYI. www.kornferry.com

Lindsay, M., Hager, Hager, M.G. 2014. View From The Top, John Wiley & Sons Inc

Maxwell, J.C., 2001. Team, Navpress

Maxwell, J.C., 2007. Be All You Can Be, Victor Books

Maxwell, J.C., 2005. 360 Degrees Leader, Nelson Books

Maxwell, J.C., 1995. Developing Leaders around you, Thomas Nelson Inc.

Maxwell, J.C., 1992. Ultimate Leadership, Thomas Nelson Inc.

Menkes, J., 2006. Executive Intelligence, Harper Collins Michaelson, S.W., 2007, Sun Tzu for Execution, Adams Business

Milne, J., 2000 Kwame Nkrumah A Biography, Panaf Books

Newman, B., 1997, 10 Laws of Leadership, Marvellous Bookshop

Prasad, B., 2018. Nimble, Penguin Random House

Simons, R., 2010. Seven Strategy Questions Harvard Business Press

Tracy, B., 2010 No excuse, Vanguard Press

Tracy, B.,2016 Meetings that get results, Amacom books

Tracy, B., 2001, Eat That Frog, Printcorp

Templar, R., 2010. Rules of work 2nd edn, Pearson Education 2003

Welch, J., Welch, J., 2005, Winning Harper Collins

Yeung, R.,2007. The Rules of Entrepreneurship, Marshall Cavendish Business

Yew, L.K., 2012. From third world to first: The Singapore Story 1965-2000, Marshall Cavendish Editions n